THE NATIONAL SOCIETY FOR PERFORMANCE AND INSTRUCTION (NSPI)

The National Society for Performance and Instruction (NSPI) is the leading international association dedicated to improving productivity and performance in the workplace. Founded in 1962, NSPI represents over ten thousand members throughout the United States and Canada and in thirty-three other countries. NSPI members work in over three thousand businesses, governmental agencies, academic institutions, and other organizations. Monthly meetings of over sixty different chapters provide professional development, services, and information exchange.

NSPI members include performance technologists, training directors, human resource managers, instructional technologists, human factors practitioners, and organizational development consultants. They are business executives, professors, line managers, government leaders, and military commanders. They work in a variety of areas: the armed forces, financial services, government agencies, health services, high technology, manufacturing, telecommunications, travel and hospitality, and universities. NSPI members are leaders in their fields and work settings. They are strategy-oriented, quality-focused, and results-centered.

The mission of NSPI is to improve the performance of individuals and organizations through the application of Human Performance Technology (HPT). NSPI's vision for itself is to be the preferred source of information, education, and advocacy for enhancing individual and organizational effectiveness, and to be respected for the tangible and enduring impact it is having on people, organizations, and the field of performance technology.

NSPI makes a difference to people by helping them grow into skilled professionals who use integrated and systematic approaches to add value to their organizations and the profession. Whether designing training programs, building selection or incentive systems, assisting organizations in their own redesign, or performing myriad other interventions, NSPI members produce results.

NSPI makes a difference to organizations by increasing professional competence and confidence. NSPI members help organizations anticipate opportunities and challenges and develop powerful solutions that contribute to productivity and satisfaction.

NSPI makes a difference to the field of performance technology by expanding the boundaries of what we know about defining, teaching, supporting, and maintaining skilled human performance. With a healthy respect for research and development, a variety of technologies, and collegial interaction, NSPI members use approaches and systems that ensure improved productivity and a better world.

For additional information, contact:

National Society for Performance and Instruction
1300 L Street, N.W., Suite 1250
Washington, DC 20005
Telephone: (202) 408-7969
Fax: (202) 408-7972

DESIGNING CROSS-FUNCTIONAL BUSINESS PROCESSES

A PUBLICATION IN THE NSPI SERIES

From Training to Performance in the Twenty-First Century

Kenneth H. Silber, Series Editor

Titles in the Series

Set 1:
DESIGNING THE WORK ENVIRONMENT FOR OPTIMUM PERFORMANCE
Elaine Weiss, Topic Editor

CREATING THE ERGONOMICALLY SOUND WORKPLACE
Lee T. Ostrom

CREATING WORKPLACES WHERE PEOPLE CAN THINK
Phyl Smith and Lynn Kearny

MAKING COMPUTERS PEOPLE-LITERATE
Elaine Weiss

Set 2:
REDESIGNING WORK PROCESSES
Judith A. Hale, Topic Editor

DESIGNING WORK GROUPS, JOBS, AND WORK FLOW
Toni Hupp with Craig Polak and Odin Westgaard

DESIGNING CROSS-FUNCTIONAL BUSINESS PROCESSES
Bernard Johann

DESIGNING CROSS-FUNCTIONAL BUSINESS PROCESSES

Bernard Johann

 JOSSEY–BASS PUBLISHERS
SAN FRANCISCO

Substantial discounts on bulk quantities of Jossey-Bass books are available
to corporations, professional associations, and other organizations. For
details and discount information, contact the special sales department at
Jossey-Bass Inc., Publishers. (415) 433-1740; Fax (415) 433-0499.

For sales outside the United States, please contact your local Paramount
Publishing International Office.

Library of Congress Cataloging-in-Publication Data

Johann, Bernard, date.
    Designing cross-functional business processes / Bernard Johann. —1st ed.
       p.   cm.—(From training to performance in the twenty-first
century. Set 2, Redesigning work processes)
    Includes bibliographical references and index.
    ISBN 0-7879-0064-8
    1. Performance technology. 2. Employees—Training of. I. Title. II. Series.
HF5549.5.P37J64   1995
658.3' 124—dc20   94-39000

PB Printing 10 9 8 7 6 5 4 3 2 1   FIRST EDITION

THE JOSSEY-BASS
MANAGEMENT SERIES

CONTENTS

From Training to Performance in the Twenty-First Century: Introduction to the Book Series   xi

Redesigning Work Processes: About This Group of Books   xvii

Preface   xix

The Author   xxiii

Section One   How Business Process Design Affects Performance   1

Overview   1

Chapter 1   Building the Case for Redesign   *3*

Section Two   Techniques for Designing Business Processes   25

Overview   25

Chapter 2   Establishing Clear Goals for Process Redesign   *31*

Chapter 3   Understanding How the Current Process Works—and Doesn't Work   *55*

Chapter 4   Creating the Simplest Possible Design to Solve the Business Problem   *103*

Chapter 5   Overcoming Barriers to Implementation   *149*

Section Three   Process Redesign in Action   161

Overview   161

Chapter 6   Speeding Up High-Tech Product Development: Case Study of Fundamental Redesign   *163*

Chapter 7   Reducing the Cost of Point-of-Purchase Displays: Case Study of Incremental Redesign   *189*

Section Four   Resources   199

Overview   199

A.   Critical Issue Worksheet   *201*

B.   Design Team Charter Worksheet   *202*

C.   Current Process Worksheet   *203*

D.   Current Culture Survey   *204*

E.   Financial and Human Resource Systems Analysis Survey   *206*

F.   Process Analysis Worksheet   *207*

G.   Customer Needs Worksheet   *211*

H.   Worksheet for Choosing Incremental or Fundamental
     Resdesign   *213*

I.   Accomplishments and Activities Worksheet   *214*

J.   Performance Gap Analysis Worksheet   *215*

K.   Cost/Benefit Analysis Worksheet   *216*

L.   Implementation Worksheet   *218*

References   *219*

Index   *223*

From Training to Performance in the Twenty-First Century: Introduction to the Book Series

For most trainers and instructional developers, the following request from a client sounds familiar: "I have a problem. Give me some training to solve it." We are taught to think that training is the answer to most human performance problems. But those of us who are veterans in the field have learned from our own experience and from others' research and theories that most of the problems our clients bring us are *not* best solved by training, or require some other solution in addition to training. What do we do in the face of this contradictory evidence?

We change our view of the world, our paradigm for thinking about how to solve our customers' problems. We look at practitioners in other fields and see how they recommend solving problems, and we try to incorporate their ideas and interventions into our own "bag of tricks."

We have heard and read about a wide array of such interventions: human-computer interface and workplace design; work process reengineering and sociotechnical systems; job aids, expert systems, and performance support systems; motivation, incentive, and feedback systems; organizational design, cultural change, and change management; measurement of results to demonstrate bottom-line savings. How do all these interventions fit together? Is there a field that incorporates and relates them? Yes. It is called Human Performance Technology (HPT).

What is human performance technology?

What makes HPT different from training, management consulting, and other practices aimed at improving the performance of people and organizations? According to Foshay and Moller (1992, p. 702), HPT is unique because it is "an applied field, not a discipline. it is structured primarily by the real world problem of human performance (in the workplace). It draws from any discipline that has prescriptive power in solving any human performance problem." Stolovitch and Keeps (1992, p. 7) have incorporated a variety of definitions of the field into their descriptions of HPT's unique approach to synthesizing ideas borrowed from other disciplines:

> *HPT, therefore, is an engineering approach to attaining desired accomplishments from human performers. HP technologists are those who adopt a systems view of performance gaps, systematically analyze both gap and system, and design cost-effective and efficient interventions that are based on analysis data, scientific knowledge, and documented precedents, in order to close the gap in the most desirable manner.*

Rummler and Brache (1992, p. 34) explain that the view HP technologists have of "what is going on . . . in organizations" is "fundamentally different" from views held by practitioners in other disciplines. HP technologists conceptualize "what is going on" by looking at and assessing three levels of variables that affect individual and organizational performance: the organization level, the work process level, and the job/worker level.

An HP technologist looks first at the total organization and at such variables as strategy and goals, structure, measurements, and management (see Figure P.1). Next, an HP technologist looks at work processes carried out across functions within the organization and analyzes the goals, design, measurement, and management of those processes to determine their effectiveness (see Figure P.2). Finally, an HP technologist looks at the job and the performer, focusing on five variables (Rummler and Brache, 1992, pp. 35–41):

1. *The performer.* Does the person have the physical, mental, and emotional ability as well as the skills and knowledge needed to perform?

2. *Inputs to the performer.* Are the available job procedures and work flow, information, money, tools, and the work environment adequate to support the desired performance?

3. *Outputs of the performer.* Do performance specifications for the outputs exist, and is the performer aware of them?

4. *Consequences of the performer's actions.* Are consequences designed to support the performance and delivered in a timely manner?

5. *Feedback the performer receives about the performance.* Does the performer receive feedback, and if so, is it relevant, timely, accurate, and specific?

Figure P.3 illustrates the relationship between these principles.

Figure P.1. The Systems View of Work.

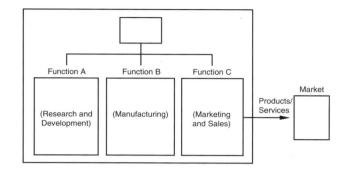

Source: Rummler and Brache, 1992, p. 35.

Figure P.2. The Cross-Functional View of Work Processes.

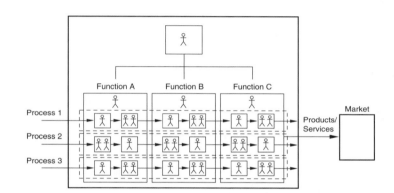

Source: Rummler and Brache, 1992, p. 37

Figure P.3. The Job/Performer View of Work.

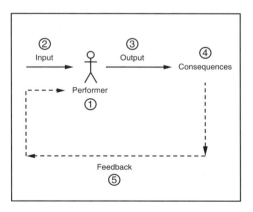

Source: Rummler and Brache, 1992, p. 38.

Purpose of the series

Once we have changed our worldview and accepted the notion of HPT interventions into our paradigm of how to approach the resolution of clients' problems, we would really like to try to implement some of them. But how?

1. Instruction is not the answer to every challenge in the workplace.

2. There are a wide array of interventions that can be used to enhance performance. . .

3. The HP technologist cannot be expected to be an expert in every intervention . . . [Rossett, 1992, p. 98].

As Rossett points out, it is not feasible for us to be experts in all these interventions. First, because the fields from which the interventions come are so diverse and constantly changing, it is virtually impossible for any of us to learn everything about and keep current in all fields. Second, there are very few resources out there to help us design and implement performance-enhancing interventions. Most books on the subject focus on what the interventions are and why they are important, but contain precious few specific guidelines, procedures, or rules for how to actually carry out the interventions.

So, as practitioners we face several gaps: between our grounding in the "training" field and the recognition that we need to expand our worldview to include other performance-enhancing interventions; between our desire to learn about the other interventions and the difficulty of keeping current in all the fields from which they derive; and between the desire to try performance-enhancing interventions and the lack of specific, practical guidance on how to do so.

The series From Training to Performance in the Twenty-First Century tries to bridge these gaps. First, the series is based on two assumptions: (1) that training/instructional design/HPT practitioners are, for the most part, currently limited to implementing training interventions in the workplace, and (2) that most practitioners recognize the need to broaden their worldview and range of interventions to embrace the approach described above. The series is designed to serve as a bridge from training to other areas of HPT.

Second, the series is a *translation/how-to-do-it* series that tracks down and summarizes the knowledge base of the fields from which the performance-enhancing interventions are derived and focuses on specific, practical, *how-to* techniques for implementing performance-enhancing interventions in real job situations.

Organization of the series

To accomplish our purposes, we have organized the series into manageable chunks called Sets, each comprising two to five books that address a related set of performance-enhancing interventions. Each book covers one performance-enhancing intervention completely.

To implement the translation/how-to-do-it approach, maintain consistency across the series, and make the procedures as easy as possible to learn and use, each book makes extensive use of procedure and decision tables, forms, examples (both successful and unsuccessful), and case studies. Each book begins with a brief synthesis of the theoretical foundations of the intervention, acknowledging different points of view where they exist. This introductory material is followed by chapters containing a wide variety of procedures that show how to implement each intervention step by step. Many job aids and forms are provided. The book presents one or more real-world case studies showing the entire intervention in practice, complete with filled-out forms. It also provides a resource section that contains blank forms for reproduction. Finally, an extensive bibliography covers almost all the current thinking about the intervention.

Audience

The From Training to Performance series is designed for three audiences. The primary audience is trainers, training managers, and novice HPT practitioners, who will use the books as an on-the-job reference and work tool as they move from applying training solutions to using performance improvement interventions. The second audience is longtime instructional design and HPT practitioners, who will use the books for continuing education in performance improvement interventions that have evolved since they joined the field. The third audience is graduate students in training, instructional design, performance technology, organizational development, human resource development, and management, who will use the books to learn HPT techniques.

Each audience will use the series slightly differently. Trainers and training managers might want to begin with the case studies to see how the intervention really works, then go to the procedures and forms to try out the interventions. Graduate students will almost certainly begin with the theoretical material and integrate it into their schema of HPT before moving on to apply the procedures and forms to real-world or simulated performance problems. Veteran HPT practitioners might use either of the approaches, jumping back and forth between the procedures, case study and theory, or focusing on the design and usability of the procedures and forms that are of particular professional interest to them.

It is the fervent hope of the National Society for Performance and Instruction (NSPI) that readers will use the books in this series as a continuing source of self-development, training for others, and, most important, on-the-job reference tools, to provide clients with the most cost-effective and efficient interventions for solving their business problems.

Acknowledgments

This series would not exist without the help and support of the following people, who helped create and nurture it: the late Paul Tremper, NSPI's executive director from 1985 to 1993, who provided vision and emotional support for the series and expert handling of the seemingly infinite details associated with the series at NSPI; Maurice Coleman, vice president of research and development at NSPI in 1991, and the 1991 publications committee, whose idea it was to create the series: Esther Powers (1991 NSPI president), Roger Addison (1992 NSPI president), William Coscarelli (1992 vice president of publications), and Kathleen Whiteside (1993 NSPI president), who led their boards of directors in providing emotional and financial support for the series from the beginning to the present; the topic editors and authors of the series, who through vision, intelligence, and perseverance transformed the idea of the series into the book you are now reading; Sarah Polster, editor of the management series at Jossey-Bass, who taught us what the business of publishing was all about, helped formulate the final look, feel, and chapter structure, negotiated the sometimes rough waters between our dreams about the series and what could actually be done, and coordinated the learning everyone at both NSPI and Jossey-Bass did about working together and producing a state-of-the-art series using state-of-the-art technology; Barbara Hill at Jossey-Bass, who coordinated all the deadlines, manuscripts, authors, reviews, and many other things we're glad not to have known about; Judith A. Hale, President, Hale Associates, who saw the value of the series and my involvement in it and continually and generously supported my efforts.

Dedication

This series is dedicated to a forgotten leader in the HPT field and in NSPI: the 1963 "Man of the Year in Programming," whose ideas formed the early basis for HPT's processes and interventions; a visionary who challenged the status quo, always with logic, reason, and passion; a teacher, guide, and friend who pushed his students to exemplary performance, encouraged them also to challenge the status quo, assisted them in their journey, and then rewarded their successes lavishly. The series is dedicated to the late James D. Finn, with respect and thanks for all he gave to me personally as my mentor, to those (too numerous to mention) who knew and worked with him, and to the field and profession of Human Performance Technology.

Chicago, Illinois   Kenneth H. Silber
January 1994   Series Editor

Redesigning Work Processes: About This Group of Books

What is the purpose of these books?

- "Management wants us to get the work out faster. Well, it won't get any faster as long as the process is 'hurry up, wait, and then do it again.'"

- "Management wants Marketing and Engineering to work together more efficiently. Well, they can't be efficient if they keep doing each other's work instead of what needs to be done."

- "Don't those instructional designers know something about finding out what people really do? Maybe they can help us analyze processes too."

- "Don't trainers know how to facilitate groups? Why don't we put one of them on the team charged to redesign our process?"

These statements reflect organizations' increasing awareness that processes affect productivity, and their growing expectation that trainers can contribute valuable skills to the process redesign.

The term *process* is used to represent all the activities that must happen to produce a product or offer a service. A process is how things get done, whether by people, machines, or both. Processes are not always designed. They may be a hodge-podge of activities that evolved over time in response to immediate pressures and personal work preferences. How work gets done may reflect an organization's needs rather than its customer's needs. A process is designed when there is a purposeful examination of what must happen and how to best do what is required to satisfy customer needs.

The two books in this group will prepare the reader to purposefully examine processes and identify what is needed to make those processes more efficient and effective. Both books provide a model that trainers and instructional technologists may use to leverage their already strong job and task analysis, facilitation, and project management skills.

How do these books fit in the series?

The two books in this group are a subset of the series From Training to Performance in the Twenty-First Century. They focus on how to describe, analyze, and redesign processes. They give readers the procedures and guidelines they need to be knowledgeable participants on process redesign teams.

Designing Work Groups, Jobs, and Work Flow, by Toni Hupp (with Craig Polak and Odin Westgaard), provides a basic understanding of how to describe, analyze, and redesign processes used by intact work groups within a specific function (see Figure P.4). The book will give readers a better understanding of how to identify all the activities a work group engages in. It includes procedures for capturing who does what and why, when, how, and toward what outcome they do it. It also provides procedures and guidelines for improving processes.

Figure P.4.

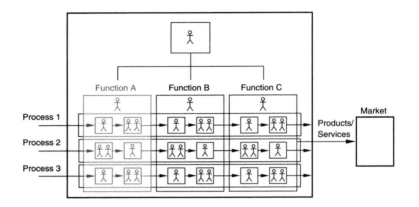

Designing Cross-Functional Business Processes, by Bernard Johann, focuses on how to identify, describe, analyze, and redesign processes that bridge traditional functional or departmental lines (see Figure P.5). It, too, includes procedures for documenting what actually happens.

It also discusses specific steps readers can follow to make incremental improvements and major redesign changes in existing processes.

Figure P.5.

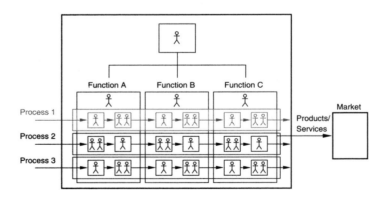

Western Springs, Illinois
January 1995

Judith A. Hale
Topic Editor

Preface

Organizational change can happen at many levels. This book focuses on one level, albeit a fundamental one.

Designing Cross-Functional Business Processes is a guide to the basic principles and methods of business process redesign. Organization effectiveness has dealt with the human side of organizational change since the 1950s. Geary Rummler and Alan Brache (1991) have talked about viewing organizations as systems, specifically in terms of the horizontal processes by which an organization produces its outputs. More recently, Michael Hammer (1990), with his background in computer sciences, talked about information systems and how we can reengineer entire corporations for significant gains in performance.

One could argue that organizational decisions are based on sound theory in economics, systems, and psychology. We must consider each of these elements when we begin to talk about improving an organization's performance through business process redesign. The relationship between the economic, systems, and human elements needs to be understood and managed if we intend to succeed at process redesign. This book offers specific tools that will help you redesign business processes by understanding and managing these three elements. This book is an attempt to bring an alternative perspective to this topic.

Background of the book

With a background in business and organizational psychology, Bernard Johann has been interested in understanding the interplay of these variables within organizations for many years. He has been especially interested in using systems thinking to improve business performance. He started by focusing on small organizations, trying to understand the basic elements of a business system. Small businesses are fertile ground for systems research. They deal firsthand with economics on a daily basis (in their cash flow), customers touch every part of the operation, information systems are usually in an embryonic state, and the variables affecting human performance are directly observable. In small business people must become systems thinkers if they want to survive. They must constantly look at the whole and how all the elements fit together.

Having also spent several years in large corporations, Johann has learned that the same variables are at play in large corporations as well. The system may be more complex and on a much larger scale, but the basic elements are quite similar. Process redesign is one of the few business improvement tools that looks at the relationships among many elements. This book tries to bring process redesign even further by bringing a true systems perspective to the topic.

Audience

Designing Cross-Functional Business Processes is the first book to provide specific tools for business process design, based on economic, systems, and psychological theory. Therefore, it offers benefits to everyone. Performance technologists can use the theory-based procedures to diagnose and solve performance problems as well as to become valuable contributors to any process design team. Organizational effectiveness practitioners can use the book to help manage change. Managers and executives can educate themselves about process design and begin to think about their organization as a series of interdependent steps, or processes. Once they recognize this interdependence, managers can diagnose problems with the entire process and begin to develop solutions that will bring noticeable improvements to their business—improvements that attack root causes, improvements customers will notice.

Overview of the book

Designing Cross-Functional Business Processes is organized into four sections.

Section One (Chapter 1) contains an introduction to the basic principles of process redesign and how to manage a business process redesign effort. A redesign effort can be broken down into four stages: clarify the request, understand the current system, create the new design, and implement the design. Each of these stages needs to be in place for process redesign to succeed.

Section Two (Chapters 2–5) details procedures for each of the four stages described above. These procedures will help you

- Clarify and understand the critical business issue that has led to process redesign
- Delve into the current operations of your organization to learn how work currently gets done
- Design a new process that will address the critical business issue and help your organization satisfy its customers
- Implement the process in a way that maximizes its success

Section Three (Chapters 6–7) presents case studies of the two different types of process redesign, fundamental and incremental redesign.

Section Four contains blank worksheets you can use in your own redesign efforts.

Acknowledgments

I would like to thank NSPI for recognizing the importance of performance technology in business process redesign; Ken Silber for keeping all of us headed in the right direction; Craig Polak for making sure what I wrote made sense; and Judith Hale for her support, expertise, and guidance.

I also want to thank my parents, who instilled in me the importance of always learning; Dagmar, my wife, who dealt with many evenings and weekends of writing; and colleagues who, through their guidance and teaching, have helped me develop as a professional.

Tempe, Arizona   Bernard Johann
January 1995

The Author

Bernard Johann is a senior business consultant for Motorola Corporation in Phoenix, Arizona. There he focuses on improving organizational performance through the systematic analysis of human performance issues and through work process redesign. He is also currently group champion, helping a $1 billion organization reduce its new-product-development cycle time. Prior to his job at Motorola he worked as a consultant with American Consulting & Training, a performance technology consulting firm; as a management consultant at Deloitte & Touche, a "big six" accounting firm; and as a manager in a small welding supply company.

Johann holds an M.A. and a Ph.D. in organizational psychology from the California School of Professional Psychology, and an M.B.A. from the College of Notre Dame. Prior to moving to Arizona, he was on the faculty of the University of California's Berkeley Extension and was a regular guest lecturer at the University of San Francisco and the College of Notre Dame. He has published several articles and a book chapter on productivity improvement, organizational culture, and human behavior in organizations.

Series Editor

Kenneth H. Silber, an associate at Hale Associates, has been contributing to the performance technology and instructional design fields since their beginnings thirty years ago. He has worked in corporate, non-profit, academic, and consulting settings internationally, designing and implementing performance improvement interventions. Silber's interventions have assisted numerous management, sales, and technical professionals with the deployment of new systems, new work processes, and new quality processes, all supported by business rationales that justify the interventions to upper management.

Silber has worked with clients to align strategic plans and product/service mixes with corporate directions and customer requirements; to reengineer work processes to reduce cycle time and costs while improving customer responsiveness; to do needs assessments and eliminate or redirect ineffective and inappropriate training; to design solutions to improve performance through environmental, technological, job-aid, work process, works standards development and documentation, certification, and feedback/motivation interventions. Before coming to Hale, Silber worked at Governors State University, AT&T, ASI/DELTAK/ALI, and Amoco. Both as a professor and a consultant, he has trained over one thousand workers to do process reengineering, peformance improvement, needs assessment, and instructional design.

Silber is a nationally recognized and published author and professional leader. He has coauthored three books, including the International Board of Standards for Training, Performance & Instructions (IBSTPI) *Instructional Design: The Standards.* A fourth book, *Training That Works: How to Train Anybody to Do Anything,* is currently in press. He started and edited the *Journal of Instructional Development,* wrote chapters for the American Society for Training and Development's (ASTD) *Training and Development Handbook* and NSPI's *Handbook of Human Performance Technology,* and has published over fifty other articles and monographs. A former member of the Executive Committee of the Association for Educational Communications and Technology (AECT) and of IBSTPI, Silber has also served as past president of the Chicago chapter of NSPI.

Silber holds a Ph.D. in instructional technology from the University of Southern California (1969) and a B.A. from the University of Rochester (1965).

Topic Editor

Judith A. Hale has been a consultant to business for over twenty years. The founder of Hale Associates, she has worked with companies to develop and improve work processes in manufacturing, customer service, assessment, and people development. Her work is recognized as innovative and practical. Her firm has developed new approaches to strategic planning, competence assessment, process design, leadership development, team building, and certification.

Hale has developed a process that training functions can use to evaluate how well they assess customer needs, provide leadership on learning and performance improvement issues, establish measures, qualify instructors, and design, develop, and deliver instructional programs. The process complements those used in ISO 9000 certifications and the Baldrige Award. It will be used by the International Board of Standards to certify training departments, instructors, instructional designers, and instructional products. Her book *How to Apply the Quality Principles to Training,* currently in press, includes procedures to evaluate how well training's processes follow the standards espoused by ISO and Baldrige.

Hale is a member of the American Society for Training and Development (ASTD) and the National Society of Performance and Instruction (NSPI). She was president of the International Board of Standards for Training, Performance, and Instruction (IBSTPI); the Chicago chapter of the Industrial Relations Research Association (IRRA); and the Chicago chapter of the National Society of Performance and Instruction (CNSPI). She was a commercial arbitrator with the American Arbitration Association and an assistant professor of communications for six years. The Insurance School of Chicago acknowledged her fourteen years of excellence to management education with its "Outstanding Educator" award in 1986. NSPI recognized her contributions to the profession with its "Outstanding Member of the Year" award in 1987.

Hale holds a Ph.D. in instructional technology from Purdue University (1991), an M.A. in communications from Miami University (1965), and a B.A. in communications from Ohio State University (1963).

HOW BUSINESS PROCESS DESIGN AFFECTS PERFORMANCE

Overview

What is this section about?

This section offers a theoretical framework for considering the need for business process redesign in today's worldwide economy. The principal rationale behind redesigning business processes is to improve organizational performance and increase customer satisfaction. The mental model (key assumption) this book follows is that business organizations are systems, and therefore "systems thinking" will generate results that traditional analyses do not.

The book further assumes that systems are composed of processes—with inputs, activities, feedback, and outcomes. Processes can be optimized only through a comprehensive understanding of the whole system. It argues that the traditional approach of fixing pieces of a process is ineffective, and recommends instead a cross-functional systems-oriented approach.

This section includes a discussion of important factors to consider during each stage of business process redesign. It prescribes a four-phase Process Redesign Model:

1. Clarify the critical business need and the metrics of success.

2. Understand how the current process works (and doesn't work).

3. Design a new process.

4. Implement and evaluate the redesigned process.

How is this section organized?

To find out:	Read these topics:	Page
What this book will do for you	Why should I read this book?	3
What today's organizational environment looks like	Why every business should think redesign	3
Why a new view of organizations is necessary	What we now know	5
Why attention must shift from parts to systems	A mental model of organizations	6
The choices facing organizations	The bottom line	6
What components to examine when looking at a work group's local system	The process view of organizations	7
The three major components of a process	A well-designed process	8
Why a new way of thinking is critical to process improvement	The case for reengineering	9
If incremental or fundamental redesign is needed	Clarifying the request— why is it important?	11
How pieces fit into the processes and how processes fit into systems	Understanding the current system—why is it important?	15
The importance of simplicity and the customer in the design phase	Creating the new design—why is it important?	17
The role of the executive	Implementing the new design—why is it important?	18
The critical and subordinate variables of successful redesign efforts	Key factors for ensuring process redesign success	19

CHAPTER 1

Building the Case for Redesign

Why Should I Read This Book?

Business process design is currently a popular topic; there are many new articles and books about it appearing every day. So why would anyone want to read yet another book on this topic? Well, there is one very good reason to read this book: it tells you *how* to redesign business processes. It gives you the tools you need to become part of a redesign team and to truly add value to an organization. It allows you to ask the "smart" questions.

Specifically, this book focuses on one particular type of business process—the cross-functional process. For example, in a new-product-development process (from product conception to product shipment), marketing assesses the market for a new product, research and development designs the product, manufacturing produces the product, sales sells the product, and customer support helps customers with after-sales service. The end result depends upon the coordinated efforts of a number of groups performing discrete functions. A successful redesign must address each of the cross-functional process's components.

Why Every Business Should Think Redesign

On October 17, 1994, *Business Week* published its 65th Anniversary Issue, titled "Rethinking Work: the economy is changing, jobs are changing, the workforce is changing. Is America ready?" This suggests a fundamental change in the contemporary global business climate and how we think about work.

Historically, a business's location and production capacity had more to do with its market share than the quality or price of its products. If a company was big enough and was located in the right place, it could manufacture products according to its own internal specifications and sell them at a price it felt was fair. But today, cheap worldwide transportation, almost instantaneous communications, and the emergence of a service economy have made this sort of attitude deadly for its adherents.

If a company doesn't understand and respond to these new forces, it is in deep trouble. Businesses must become more sophisticated in almost every way in order to maintain their position. Gerd Gerken (1990), futurist and marketing consultant, suggests that to become a leader in the area of speed, for example (i.e., to react quickly to market forces), a company must separate itself from market needs and instead work "in front of the need." In other words, when a market need becomes apparent, it is already too late.

Why business organizations are unable to respond

Unfortunately, business organizations find themselves unable to respond to such pressures. There are two basic reasons for this: One is organizational inertia, which is addressed later in this chapter. The other is bureaucracy. Any company of over a dozen or so employees begins to bureaucratize itself. The company increasingly takes on people who don't contribute directly to its productivity but who are used to support those who do. This tendency is okay to an extent. Highly productive people can be made even more productive if they don't have to attend to nonproductive tasks such as keeping records, administering programs, or attending to ancillary duties. Thus, in most organizations people are hired to help and support others. However, in some organizations the support staff, or bureaucracy, grows to an extent that it outnumbers the production staff by a large margin. Just think of the expense, both in time and money, generated by such a bureaucracy. Support staff generally cost a great deal of money, and they add processing time to production.

This discussion might lead you to think the problem is mainly one of size. This is not so. While it's true that bureaucracies tend to flourish best in large organizations, large companies have advantages that small ones can't duplicate. They command much more expertise than their smaller competitors, and they have proportionally greater capabilities. However, their customers are paying a high price for those advantages, and they are beginning to seek alternatives.

What large companies don't have is the flexibility and adaptability they must have to be competitive in today's environment. They are trying. The media report evidence of their efforts almost daily. We see large corporations "downsizing" or "restructuring" or "diversifying." Too many companies think that the easiest way to cut costs (and thereby increase profits) is to cut people. Unfortunately, unless they reengineer their operations, such drastic moves don't solve any real problems. They still don't have the flexibility and adaptability they need.

What We Now Know

The historical roots of focusing on the pieces versus the whole can be traced to the seventeenth century, to the dawn of the machine age. Isaac Newton was the first to describe the world in mechanistic terms. In this worldview it is the parts, not the whole, that are of primary interest: the properties of the parts will determine the functioning of the whole, like in a machine. Today, we are beginning instead to look at the unique properties of the whole—the system—and their effect on its components. Margaret Wheatley (1992) offers a succinct explanation of the difference between these two worldviews:

> In the machine model, one must understand parts. Things can be taken apart, dissected literally or representationally (as we have done with business functions and academic disciplines), and then put back together without any significant loss. The assumption is that by comprehending the workings of each piece, the whole can be understood. The Newtonian model of the world is characterized by materialism and reductionism—a focus on things rather than relationships and a search, in physics, for the basic building blocks of matter. In new science, the underlying currents are a movement toward holism, toward understanding the system as a system and giving primary value to the relationships that exist among the seemingly discrete parts.

Mechanistic model problems

The mechanistic model no longer suffices in today's world. As Hammer and Champy (1993) point out, the problems associated with it are rampant:

- Slow response time
- A bureaucratic structure
- Increased expenses
- Lower productivity
- Slower decision making
- Smaller cash flow
- Decreased ability to stay competitive
- Human costs (absenteeism, turnover, cynicism, low productivity)

The new model

The new model is that of the quantum world. Compared with the order and hierarchical nature of the mechanistic world, the quantum world is chaotic, unpredictable. And the organizational researcher's role has shifted from one of examining jobs, departments, or functions to one of analyzing the relationships between these elements.

A Mental Model of Organizations

Organizational theorists and designers have begun to see organizations as complex systems that continually adapt to change (Mackenzie, 1989). Some suggest that organizations are living systems, whose purpose is to create a viable existence (Beer, 1985). These new models stress the importance of relationships and interdependencies, as Wheatley (1992) explains:

> We need to learn more about this "interweaving of processes" that leads to structure. In ways we have never noticed, the whole of a system manages itself as a total system through natural processes that maintain its integrity. It is critical that we see these processes. It will shift our attention away from the parts, those rusting holdovers from an earlier age of organization, and focus us on the deeper, embedded processes that create whole organizations (p. 118).

Organizational inertia

In his seminal work on the psychology of organizations, Kurt Lewin (1947) offers this explanation of the tendency of organizations to bog down in familiar patterns: When a person encounters a difficulty, he or she tries to avoid it or overcome it. If successful, the person remembers the tactic used, and the next time a difficulty comes along he or she tries the same tactic again. If success again follows, the tactic is made even more a part of his or her repertoire. In essence it becomes the tactic of choice for any eventuality. People in organizations also behave in this way. All have their favorite tactics, and each tries to use the preferred approach whenever he or she encounters a problem. In any organization, large or small, people use their favored tactics to overcome difficulties. The sum total of all this effort has been called organizational inertia. It's like the concept of inertia in physics—an object in motion tends to maintain its direction and force until it's redirected. The same is true of organizations. And the larger the organization or the longer its particular tactics have been successful, the stronger its inertia.

The Bottom Line

Stop for a moment and think about the implications of these new organizational models. What does all this mean to business people? What does it imply for you? Should you throw up your hands and stop trying? Of course not.

The fundamental truth is that there has never been a greater opportunity. We have the chance, now, to achieve incredible new vistas of success. The world is coming together as a cohesive entity. Trade barriers are going down. Communication is not only easier, it's becoming more meaningful. People with vision haven't waited to get started. McDonald's is selling hamburgers in more than seventy countries. IBM has mainframe systems in place all over the world. Oil companies like British Petroleum and Dutch Shell have market outlets everywhere. Intel provides computer chips to the world. CNN broadcasts in almost every country. Motorola sells cellular telephones worldwide.

Every country, every region, every city and village is included. Every human being on earth is a potential customer. But, as noted above, you can't take advantage of these opportunities using the old ways of producing products and services. You must change or accept a lesser role.

There are basically three choices:

1. You can continue as before, hoping to maintain enough productivity to survive for as long as you deem necessary.

2. You can modify your existing environment to make it more efficient, more effective, and (if possible) capable of producing higher-quality goods or services.

3. You can literally junk your current way of doing things and reinvent yourself.

The Process View of Organizations

A *process* is "how" we get things done. Consider the manufacture of a radio. The "what" is a finished radio in the hands of a customer. The "how" is all the steps involved in getting it there: procurement, design, marketing, manufacturing, shipping, distribution, invoicing, and whatever else is necessary. When you think about it, process is what defines an organization: true, the organization may ultimately manufacture goods, or provide services, or support other organizations, but essentially those products and services are the outcomes of a process or processes. They are the artifacts of the organization's efforts, indicators of the efficacy of the processes it uses.

The key difference to the approach this book advocates is that it requires managers to embrace the idea that their operation is a process. It's to your advantage to learn to think of what your unit does in terms of the process it involves. Instead of making a product, for example, think of your unit as assembling the parts according to a predetermined system. The difference may not sound like much, but it can be crucial, particularly when you're attempting to change the way you accomplish your goals.

Adopting a process view

Davenport (1993) explains the importance of adopting a process view this way:

> *Taking a process approach implies adopting the customer's point of view . . . looking at the process by which a product is produced, deemphasizing the functional structures, and emphasizing the cross-functional structures. Process innovation demands that interfaces between functional or product units be either improved or eliminated and that, where possible, sequential flows across functions be made parallel through rapid and continuous movement of information (p. 7).*

This kind of thinking is in stark contrast with the "world as a machine" model developed by Newton.

When you think of a production or service process, think of it like a stream of water. Although there are distinct activities, each flows into the next. And each activity is accompanied by others that happen at the same time. None can be separated from the others without disrupting the basic nature of the process. You might dam up the stream, but it would overflow the dam. You might put dye into it to identify specific flows, but the dye would disperse, spread out, and fade away. You might separate a drop of water to analyze it, but in doing so you would have to remove it from the stream and it would no longer represent the stream from which it came.

A well-designed process

A well-designed process has three fundamental aspects: First, it is designed from the back forward. That is, the designers begin by considering what the output is supposed to look, feel, and be like. Then they work backward through the process to design a way to produce that output. Second, a good process is efficient. It uses people well—it doesn't waste their time, skills, or energy. Third, it's effective. It produces what it is supposed to produce with optimum use of time, effort, materials, and equipment.

Rummler and Brache (1991) argue that the only way to understand how work gets done is to view the organization horizontally—by processes. They state that by managing and improving the "white" space that currently exists between departments and functions, organizations can become more effective and use resources more efficiently. Their approach of looking at the current process and then eliminating "white" space is a powerful methodology for improving an existing process. However, in many cases an organization needs to break free from its current way of thinking, its current way of doing things. It needs to reengineer or reinvent itself.

The case for reengineering

If you're thinking about improving a process, there are essentially two approaches:

1. You can redesign an existing process, but it's likely that whatever you develop will be a modification or extension of the original process. In most cases, this will not give you significant improvements in performance.

2. You can design a new process from scratch. This is known as reengineering. Think about it this way: reengineering a process requires a paradigm shift; it requires not only a new approach but a new conceptualization. Actually, it might be better to call reengineering "reinventing" because that, essentially, is what it entails.

The first lesson, then, is to understand that reengineering or reinventing a process demands a different viewpoint and, consequently, a different way of thinking. The difficulty for most people is not in understanding the need for change, it lies in being able to let go of closely held models that have worked well in the past. Techniques like process control, incremental measurement, formative feedback, quality control, troubleshooting, and so on are very valuable when the goal is to improve the function of an existing process. But when the goal is to rethink and reinvent the process, they are no longer useful.

The methodologies and teachings of Rummler and Brache don't directly apply to process reengineering. That is not to say they are not valuable. On the contrary, given a reengineered system, they become even more important: no new system is without bugs, and their model provides the best debugging process ever introduced. But the fact remains that, to be able to pursue process reengineering, you must learn a new discipline. It begins with the procedures defined by Senge (1990), Hammer (1990), and Kaufman (1992), and it culminates in your own original thoughts and practices.

Beginning process improvement

Process improvement begins with a thorough examination of the current state of things. In the case of Rummler and Brache's model, this conceptualization is called making an "is map." An important assumption is that the goal of the current system is compatible with customer expectations. When that assumption is in error (whether by a large or small degree), process mapping, process improvement, and other, similar models no longer suffice.

To understand what reengineering implies, consider the ideas promoted by Senge and those developed by Kaufman. Both base their thinking on a systemic conceptualization of the organization. Systemic thinking refers to looking at the interrelationships that influence the behavior of the organization. Senge's *Fifth Discipline* describes the use of systemic thinking, personal mastery, mental models, shared visions, and team learning to promote a holistic approach to understanding organizational efforts. Kaufman's *Strategic Planning Plus* concentrates on developing what he calls a mega approach to organizational thinking. In both cases the approach is strategic rather than tactical. It begins with an understanding of the organization as a social organism, a viable living element of a wider, universal society.

So it is appropriate to focus on the customer, if the customer represents that greater society in which the organization lives. To the mind considering reengineering organizational processes, the wants and needs of the customer are considered universal rather than insular. In other words, assume that everybody in the world requires your products or services. The trick to wisely reengineering the processes you use is to discover what this vast customer (the world) thinks you ought to provide, and *then* invent a way to provide it.

It's not easy. You must be continuously aware that success will bring major organizational changes. There will be resistance at every step of the way. Therefore, the effort must be carefully managed. You must identify and focus on a number of critical stages that constitute a redesign project.

From the Theory to the Model

The goal becomes one of balancing this theoretical grounding with the need for a practical approach to business process redesign. Practical experience, the scientific method, and trial and error led to the following four-phase Process Redesign Model:

1. Clarify the critical business need and the metrics of success.

2. Understand how the current process works (and doesn't work).

3. Design a new process.

4. Implement and evaluate the redesigned process.

1. Clarifying the request—why is it important?

It seems like an obvious first step, but it's surprising how many redesign efforts are derailed by the lack of a clearly defined goal. It is critical that you clarify the need the redesigned process will fulfill, both to help you formulate the new design and to help you assess your success after it has been implemented. Begin by following these steps:

- Determine specifically what the sponsor of the team wants to accomplish and how the organization will know that you accomplished it. The redesign methodology you use will depend not only on the charter of the team, but also on the desires of the executive in charge of the effort and the scale of improvement required to address the critical business issue.

- Assess if the executive team understands process redesign and is ready to engage in such an effort.

- Determine if and how the effort supports the organization's business strategy.

The focus at the start of any project is to come to a mutual understanding of the team's charter and the organization's expectations for the project. What is the critical business issue? What process does the organization need to fix? How will it know if it is fixed?

There are two basic methodologies for solving this critical business issue:

1. Incremental process redesign, where you start with a detailed current process map and improve the existing processes.

2. Fundamental process design (reengineering), where you start with a current process map and then design a new process from scratch to address the critical business issue at hand. After the new process has been designed, you then redesign the organization chart.

Many authors argue that focusing on incremental redesign will never work, that the organization will never achieve large increases in performance. Fixing a process, instead of changing it, will fail to achieve "really improved" business performance (Hammer and Champy, 1993). Yet, in many respects, incremental redesign can also produce continuous improvements.

Incremental versus fundamental redesign

The table below shows the significant differences between incremental and fundamental redesign. A fundamental redesign project tends to take longer, the potential improvement is larger, and the level of change required by the organization is greater.

Variable/Topic	Incremental Redesign: Process Improvement	Fundamental Redesign: Process Reengineering
Starting point	Current process map	Current process map plus a blank sheet of paper
Level of change	Incremental	Fundamental
Type of change	Cultural	Structural and cultural
Frequency of change	One time/continuous	One time
Assumptions	Work within current assumptions	Challenge existing assumptions
Executive involvement	Moderate	High
Resources	People and money	People and money
Timeline	Weeks	Twelve months to three years, depending on executive support
Participation	Bottom up	Top down
Focus/integration	Less	More
Scope	Narrow	Broad
Risk	Moderate	High
Driver	Statistical control	Information technology
Potential gain	Smaller	Larger

Adapted from Davenport (1993, p. 11)

The need for great leaps

It's important to note that fundamental change does not imply an end to ongoing, continuous improvement—companies must always strive to improve. Rather, the fundamental redesign argument is based on the assumption that to stay competitive in today's global environment, organizations need great leaps in improvement, not just tiny hops. Furthermore, since most businesses' processes were never "designed" in the first place, it's most effective to start fresh and design them.

In today's competitive environment, both types of redesign may be necessary.

One important point to clarify when beginning a process redesign is how much improvement is expected. For example, let's take a new-product-introduction process. Does management want a 10-percent improvement in development time (reducing a 100-day cycle to 90 days), or to compete does the company need a 90-percent improvement (to go from 100 days to 10 days)? These different expectations require different redesign methodologies.

The cost-to-value trade-off

Fundamental change is not always needed. There is a cost-to-value trade-off to consider. If your cycle time for a particular process is 100 days and your competition's is 90 days, you need to carefully evaluate whether radical change is necessary. Improving your process to 70 or 80 days may be all that is needed. Some companies improve their current processes incrementally while a redesign team focuses on the larger issue of redesigning entire core processes from scratch. Always keep the idea of cost versus benefit in mind.

Fundamental redesign is not easy. Even if the prototype processes function perfectly, institutionalizing the new design across the organization can be difficult. A "not-invented-here" mentality is often quite intense. People tend to have many questions. Displaced managers may ask, What happens to me now, what about my job? Those with budgetary responsibilities may be reluctant to give up decision-making authority. Redesign team members may also wonder about their careers, since these projects sometimes last several years. Therefore, the organization's measurement procedures, metrics, reward systems, evaluation methods, and career development conventions *all* need to be redesigned so as to be in alignment with the new process. Fundamental redesign is a major effort: it requires the top manager—possibly the CEO—to devote a substantial amount of his or her time.

Management's role

Often the sponsoring body is not familiar with redesign theory or methodology, and sometimes process redesign is not even mentioned. This can lead to unnecessary concern over the redesign project. Increasing inventory turns, for example, may require redesigning the entire order-to-ship process. Therefore, management must understand that the company's *processes* are to be redesigned, not its departments or functions. Only after the processes have been redesigned do you redesign the organizational chart.

To create a sense of urgency for a redesign project, top management must support the redesign effort. The case for the redesign must be compelling, urgent, clear, and constantly reinforced. This is important in incremental redesign, but it's vital in fundamental redesign.

Guiding the change effort

In fundamental redesign top management must be actively involved in guiding the change effort. When you look at an organization's processes you begin to look at the horizontal planes within the organization. They cross many functional boundaries, political fiefdoms, and so on. Often a redesigned process will shift power bases within an organization and change the dynamics of the business. If the redesign is not led by a person who has the authority to oversee a process from start to finish, the redesign effort will fall apart under political pressure and the demands of day-to-day activities.

Furthermore, top executives need to constantly restate their expectations throughout the redesign effort. When executives state their expectations so often they begin to "get sick of repeating themselves," it will create focus in the organization, encourage consistency in the redesign project's approach, and foster a sense of urgency.

Top management must have the ability to build and maintain trust within the organization. Since change tends to threaten the basic security of individuals, trust is key. Trust is cultivated when management's messages are consistent and when people consistently do what they say. It's also important to make the changes as predictable as possible. It is the ambiguity surrounding change efforts (what will happen to me now?) that causes concern.

The organization's business strategy will tell you what operations are important. The organization must have a clearly defined strategy before redesign takes place. It is the redesign team's responsibility to be clear on the business strategy and what the organization hopes to achieve. Always keep in mind that the organization should *not* fix what it should not be doing in the first place.

2. Understanding the current system—why is it important?

Just as it's vitally important to clarify the needs the redesign project will address, it's crucial that you start with a clear understanding of the current state of the system you're about to change. Understanding the current system allows you to

- Know what you are working on. How does the current process provide an output (product or service) to the customer?
- Create a common understanding between the organization and the redesign team of the problems with the current process.
- Determine how the current process affects customers.

Process stresses a horizontal view of the organization, focusing on the activities rather than functional departments necessary to get the output to the customer. Hammer and Champy (1993) cite four excellent examples of recurring processes and what they call their "state-change names":

- Product development (concept to prototype)
- Sales (prospect to order)
- Order fulfillment (order to payment)
- Customer service (inquiry to resolution)

Understanding the current process is *not* the same as analyzing it. Analysis looks only at the inputs and outputs. Understanding means questioning everything. You want to understand what the current process does, how well it performs, the variables that govern its performance, and the assumptions used to justify each of its targeted outputs or accomplishments. You must question the purpose of each input and output, and recognize that a process is a dynamic entity, changing over time. Remember that you are trying to obtain a comprehensive "snapshot" of the process at a particular point in time.

Therefore the team needs to understand the *entire* process. A core cross-functional process contains many activities and is often highly complex. This complexity often leads organizations to look at its pieces instead of the entire process. Some organizations have different teams look at different pieces of a process that's causing major problems. The risk to this approach is that in most cases these teams don't communicate. Additional time is spent coordinating teams, especially if they have different sponsors. It becomes unclear what has already been done and what is not yet done. Authority and decision-making processes become blurred. Since each team looks at the process from a different vantage point, they each obtain a different result, and no one learns how the entire process functions. Therefore, although the pieces are optimized, the overall process does not get better. Furthermore, as one part is redesigned it may negatively influence another part. There may be no change to the final output of the overall process, and the customer never notices an improvement.

A good rule of thumb is that only one core team should redesign a cross-functional process. As the project progresses, this team might sponsor subteams, but it is clear that the subteams report to the team leader of the core redesign team. Furthermore, the CEO, or a person with comparable authority over an entire cross-functional process (the sponsor of the effort), should retain full decision-making authority.

Current process map

A current process map provides a common framework, a shared understanding of how work gets done. The team needs to understand all elements of the current process and how they affect the customer. This can only be done if a team looks at the cross-functional process beginning to end. The team *and* the organization must see how "it all fits together."

Many fundamental redesign experts argue that spending too much time studying the existing system will lead to "analysis paralysis." The key is not to get bogged down. (This is important for both fundamental and incremental redesign.) The focus should always be on understanding and learning from the current processes.

Systems analysis aims to uncover how the parts relate within the whole—how one element affects the other elements in the process. For example, say you've just been asked to join a team that is going to redesign the product-development (concept to prototype) process for your company. Is the product-development process the only process you'll need to understand? Probably not. Your company's annual budget cycle, fiscal year cutoff, and financial reporting processes might significantly affect your redesign of the product-development process.

The need for systems thinking

You have to become a systems thinker. You must learn to see all the cross-functional interrelationships. You must accept that discovering the optimal way to improve a given situation depends on your understanding of other perspectives and methodologies. As Weinberg (1982) puts it, "the main trouble with analysis comes when the results drawn from one small territory are erroneously applied to another. Practitioners may forget that they are working in a small territory and begin to imagine their territory is the universe (p. 28)."

It is important for the redesign team to take an outside-in versus an inside-out approach. Outside-in means the process redesign is driven by the needs of the market and the customers. The team's ability to focus on the needs and wants of the customer throughout the entire process is critical. Many times processes are redesigned (often with dramatic internal impacts) without producing changes that matter to the customer. The team must create an environment where ideas are constantly tested against what customers want. Everyone must begin to think like the customer. The best way to ensure this happens is to

- Include customers on the team

- Lead focus groups with customers

- Have customers critique the plans and give constant feedback

As the team begins to uncover problems, people become cynical, fearful, and resistant. To help deal with these behaviors, the core team should constantly talk with customers and share these conversations with individuals inside the organization, to show them that it is customer need that is driving the redesign effort.

3. Creating the new design—why is it important?

You are now ready to develop solutions to the problems you uncovered in looking at the current system, to close the gap between the organization's expectations and its performance. You are now the designer: you understand the system, you understand its position in the wider society, and you must now design a process that meets the organization's critical business needs.

A strong dose of common sense helps. By now you undoubtedly will have experienced the organizational system's strangest behavior. For example, you might have observed an ordering process where a purchase order is first handwritten, then entered into a computer and printed, then entered into another computer system and electronically transmitted back to the person who initially wrote the order. Common sense will tell you such a process is ineffective.

In creating a new process design your team will come up with many creative ideas for solving these types of performance problems. As you design, keep two fundamental themes in mind:

- Simplicity
- Impact on the customer

The process should be as simple as possible. If the same outcome can be achieved with five steps instead of ten, use five. Constantly check to be sure your design benefits the customer. Bring the "voice of the customer" into the organization throughout the entire process. Have customers critique the new design's performance.

Rarely will one design satisfy all needs. In most cases there are several versions of a particular process. In incremental redesign, the team creates several alternative plans to best close the performance gap and then chooses which one it thinks is best. This is then presented to management. In fundamental redesign, the team uses prototypes to optimize the design. In any redesign there will be trade-offs. The team needs to be clear on what those are, communicate them to management, and let management decide what is most important to the customer.

4. Implementing the new design—why is it important?

Once the new process is designed on paper, it is time to implement it. Strong management support and reinforcement of a sense of urgency is needed to make the change happen. The redesign team and top management must both continue to stress the importance of these two goals:

- Change the way work gets done (the operations).
- Satisfy the critical business need.

Think of the new process as a "work in progress." There will always be minor glitches that need to be fixed and improved. For a fundamental redesign project, you will most likely perform a pilot study on the new process at work in a particular operation. After the pilot study, the team will need to integrate the new process into the overall operations of the organization. The redesign team will then often face resistance as well as a number of complex questions on how other functions (Human Resources, Finance, and so on) will be affected (Duck, 1993).

During implementation the hard work for the top executive begins. He or she must constantly assert his or her expectations. Communicating with members of the organization is critical. As you begin to observe the newly implemented process at work, you will doubtless discover that other changes need to be made. These need to be coordinated with top management. The redesign team may now become the transition team. With the executive as its leader, this team has the authority to allocate resources and to stop any activities that are not in sync with the overall change strategy (Duck, 1993). During implementation, you will want to bring in customers to evaluate the impact of the change and to reinforce the necessity of implementing the new process.

Key Factors for Ensuring Process Redesign Success

The success of any redesign effort depends on six major variables:

1. How clear the redesign team's charter (contract) is. Is the sponsoring executive or management body clear on its desired outcome and how it will be measured? Is the team?

2. How well the team and the steering committee are able to build trust within the organization. Many change efforts threaten the basic "security and safety" needs of individuals. Trust is a key variable that must be managed. Trust is based on predictability. People have to see how the new process will work and what the predictable consequences are.

3. How well the sponsoring executives and the redesign team communicate throughout the entire redesign effort. Do the sponsors help make things as predictable as possible? Is he or she directly involved?

4. How well the redesign team understands the current system and builds on the organization's core competencies.

5. How well the team markets, plans, and executes the redesign effort. Does the team communicate, teach, and involve the rest of the organization in redesign?

6. How well the team understands customer needs and problems. Will the new process help eliminate customer problems? What impact does the new process have on the customer?

Other critical variables in producing successful incremental and fundamental redesign are listed in the following table.

Incremental Redesign	Fundamental Redesign
The team must	The team must
• Clearly understand the performance goals and metrics of success for all elements of the process.	• Ensure that 20–60% of the top manager's time (often the CEO) is devoted to the project.
• Have strong management support.	• Set an aggressive goal. The core process to be redesigned must span the entire business. The target set must span the business unit.
• Understand the interdependencies between processes.	• Understand customer needs, market trends, and core competencies.
• Clearly communicate the goals, purpose, and progress of the redesign project.	• Ensure that one executive is responsible for implementation. The executive should spend 60% of his or her time on the redesign effort during this phase.
• Manage the psychology of change by constantly working on building and maintaining trust.	• Conduct a comprehensive pilot study of the new design.
	• Develop a comprehensive and thorough communication plan.

Column 2 is adapted from "How to Make Reengineering Really Work," *Harvard Business Review*, November–December 1993

For More Information

Bardwick, J. M. *Danger in the Comfort Zone*. New York: AMACOM, 1991.

Beer, M., Eisenstat, R. A., and Spector, B. "Why Change Programs Don't Produce Change." *Harvard Business Review* (November–December 1992): 158–166.

Beer, S. *Brain of the Firm*. New York: Penguin Press, 1972.

Beer, S. *Diagnosing the System for Organizations*. New York: Wiley, 1985.

Brethower, Dale. *Behavior Analysis in Business and Industry: The Total Performance System*. Kalamazoo, Mich: Behaviordelia, 1971.

Bridges, W. *Managing Transitions*. Reading, Mass.: Addison-Wesley, 1991.

Daniels, W. R. *Group Power I: A Manager's Guide to Using Task Force Meetings*. San Diego: Pfeiffer, 1986.

Daniels, W. R. *Group Power II: A Manager's Guide to Conducting Regular Meetings*. San Diego: Pfeiffer, 1990.

Davenport, T. H. *Process Innovation—Reengineering Work through Information Technology*. Boston, Mass.: Harvard Business School Press, 1993.

De Bono, E. *Serious Creativity*. New York: Harper Business, 1992.

Dewar, R. D. and Dutton, J. E. "The Adoption of Radical and Incremental Innovations: An Empirical Analysis." *Management Science*, 1986, *32* (11): 1422–1433.

Duck, J. D. "Managing Change: The Art of Balancing." *Harvard Business Review* (November–December 1993): 109–118.

Eisenhardt, K. "Speed and Strategic Choice: How Managers Accelerate Decision Making." *California Management Review*, 1990, *32* (Spring), 39–54.

Eureka, W. E. and Ryan, N. E. *The Customer-Driven Company*. Dearborn, Mich.: ASI Press, 1988.

Fields, R., Taylor, P., Weyler, R., and Ingrasci, R. *Chop Wood Carry Water*. Los Angeles: Jeremy P. Tarcher, Inc., 1984.

Gabarro, J. J. *The Dynamics of Taking Charge*. Boston, Mass.: Harvard Business School Press, 1987.

Galbraith, J. R. *Organization Design*. Reading, Mass.: Addison-Wesley, 1977.

Gerken, G. *Abschied vom Marketing*. Düsseldorf, Germany: ECON Verlag, 1990.

Gibb, J. *Trust*. North Hollywood, Calif.: Newcastle Publishing, 1991.

Goldratt, E. *The Goal*. Croton-on-Hudson, N.Y.: North River Press, Inc., 1984.

Hall, G., Rosenthal, J., and Wade, J. "How to Make Reengineering Really Work." *Harvard Business Review* (November–December 1993), 119–131.

Hamel, G. and Prahalad, C. K. "Strategic Intent." *Harvard Business Review* (May–June 1989): 63–76.

Hamel, G. and Prahalad, C. K. "Strategy as Stretch and Leverage." *Harvard Business Review* (March–April 1993): 75–84.

Hammer, M. "Reengineering Work: Don't Automate, Obliterate." *Harvard Business Review* (July–August 1990): 104–112.

Hammer, M. and Champy, J. *Reengineering the Corporation.* New York: HarperCollins, 1993.

Harrison, R. "Understanding Your Organization's Character." *Harvard Business Review* (May–June 1972): 119–128.

Jaques, E. *Requisite Organization.* Arlington, Va.: Cason Hall, 1989.

Juran, J. M. *Juran on Quality by Design.* New York: Free Press, 1992.

Kaplan, R. B. and Murdock, L. "Core Process Redesign." *McKinsey Quarterly*, 1991, *2*, 27–43.

Katz, D. and Kahn, R. L. *The Social Psychology of Organizations.* New York: Wiley, 1966.

Kaufman, R. *Strategic Planning Plus: An Organizational Guide.* Newbury Park, Calif.: Sage Publishing, 1992.

Langeler, G. H. "The Vision Trap." *Harvard Business Review* (March–April 1992): 46–55.

Lawler, E. E. *The Ultimate Advantage: Creating the High Involvement Organization.* San Francisco: Jossey-Bass, 1992.

Leeds, D. "The Art of Asking Questions." *Training and Development* (January 1993): 57–62.

Lewin, K. "Group Decision and Social Change." In T. Newcomb and E. Hartely (eds.), *Readings in Social Psychology.* New York: Holt, Rinehart and Winston, 1947.

Lincoln, Y. S. and Guba, E. G. *Naturalistic Inquiry.* Newbury Park, Calif.: Sage Publications, 1985.

Mackenzie, K. D. "The Process Approach to Organizational Design." *Human Systems Management*, 1989, *8*, 31–43.

Miller, J. *Living Systems.* New York: McGraw-Hill, 1978.

Mintzberg, H. *Mintzberg on Management.* New York: Free Press, 1989.

Morris, D. and Brandon, J. *Reengineering Your Business.* New York: McGraw-Hill, 1993.

Northey, P. and Southway, N. *Cycle Time Management.* Cambridge, Mass.: Productivity Press, 1993.

Pasmore, W. A. *Designing Effective Organizations—The Sociotechnical Systems Perspective.* New York: Wiley, 1988.

Perrow, C. *Organizational Analysis.* Belmont, Calif.: Wadsworth, 1970.

Phillips, D. *Lincoln on Leadership.* New York: Warner Books, 1992.

Porras, J. I. *Stream Analysis: A Powerful Way to Diagnose and Manage Organization Change.* Reading, Mass.: Addison-Wesley, 1987.

Porter, M. E. *Competitive Strategy.* New York: Free Press, 1980.

Prahalad, C. K. "The Core Competence of the Organization." *Harvard Business Review* (May–June 1990): 79–91.

Putz, B. [Johann, B.] "Guidelines to Constructing Evaluation Instruments." In F. Stein (ed.), *Instructor Competencies: The Standards* (193–223). Batavia, Ill.: International Board of Standards for Training, Performance and Instruction, 1992.

Rummler, G. A. and Brache, A. P. *Improving Performance.* San Francisco: Jossey-Bass, 1991.

Ryan, K. D. and Oestreich, D. K. *Driving Fear Out of the Workplace.* San Francisco: Jossey-Bass, 1991.

Schaffer, R. H. "Demand Better Results and Get Them." *Harvard Business Review* (March–April 1991): 142–149.

Schaffer, R. H. and Thomson, H. A. "Successful Change Programs Begin with Results." *Harvard Business Review* (January–February 1992): 80–89.

Senge, P. M. *The Fifth Discipline.* New York: Doubleday, 1990.

Shapiro, B. P., Rangan, V. K., and Sviokla, J. J. "Staple Yourself to an Order." *Harvard Business Review* (July–August 1992): 113–122.

Smith, P. G. and Reinertsen, D. G. *Developing Products in Half the Time.* New York: Van Nostrand Reinhold, 1991.

Spadaford, J. F. "Reengineering Commercial Loan Servicing at First Chicago." *National Productivity Review* (Winter 1992–93): 65–72.

Srivastva, S. *Executive Power.* San Francisco: Jossey-Bass, 1986.

Stalk, G., Evans, P., and Shulman, L. E. "Competing on Capabilities: The New Rules of Corporate Strategy." *Harvard Business Review* (March–April 1992), 57–69.

Stolovitch, H. D. and Keeps, E. J., eds. *Handbook of Human Performance Technology.* San Francisco: Jossey-Bass, 1992.

Tichy, N. M. and Sherman, S. *Control Your Destiny or Someone Else Will.* New York: Doubleday, 1993.

Tomasko, R. M., *Rethinking the Corporation: The Architecture of Change.* New York: AMACOM, 1993.

Umbaugh, R. E. *Handbook of IS Management.* Boston: Auerbach, 1991.

Umbaugh, R. E. *Handbook of IS Management: 1993–1994 Yearbook.* Boston: Auerbach, 1993.

VanGundy, J., *Techniques of Structured Problem Solving.* New York: Van Nostrand Reinhold, 1988.

Walker, R. "Rank Xerox—Management Revolution." *Long Range Planning,* 1992, *25* (February), 7–21.

Weinberg, G. M. *Rethinking Systems Analysis and Design.* Boston: Little, Brown, 1982.

Wheatley, M. J. *Leadership and the New Science.* San Francisco: Berrett-Koehler, 1992.

Wurman, R. S. *Information Anxiety.* New York: Doubleday, 1989.

TECHNIQUES FOR DESIGNING BUSINESS PROCESSES

Overview

Give us the tools, and we will finish the job. Churchill, 1941

Purpose of this section

This section describes procedures that will help you achieve the kind of end result you read about in Section One. The procedures will help you diagnose, initiate, and manage a redesign project. Given the magnitude of these projects, redesign is not accomplished by a single individual. There is almost always a redesign team, with a clear charter and sponsor. The procedures described in this section will help you to become a valuable contributor to the redesign team. As your team works on a project, you can guide and influence it using the methods described in this section.

Whether you engage in incremental process redesign or fundamental process redesign, the basic steps are essentially the same: clarify the request, understand the current system, create the new design, and implement the new design. The only difference is in how the steps are performed. The table on the next page summarizes how the basic steps are similar or different as they are applied to the two different redesign types.

Chapter	Similar or Different?	Incremental Redesign	Fundamental Redesign	Summary
2—Clarifying the request	Different	Clarifying the request is critical in incremental redesign. The charter is focused on a minor change effort.	Clarifying the request is critical in fundamental redesign. The charter is focused on a major change effort.	Although some of the same techniques are used, the charter is quite different. If you don't get top management's involvement, fundamental redesign will not succeed. The overall change effort will be very different depending on the type of redesign.
3—Understanding the current system	Similar	You need to fully understand the current process before you can make any changes.	You need to fully understand the current process before you can make any changes.	In both types of redesign you need to have a thorough understanding of the current process and the current system before you begin. Therefore, whether you engage in incremental redesign or fundamental redesign, the activities are similar.
4—Creating the new design	Different	You are improving only elements of an existing process.	You are creating a completely new process.	You may use similar procedures to identify where the process is not functioning efficiently and to identify alternatives; however, in fundamental redesign you have more liberty to challenge the status quo. Consequently, the way you design the new process is different than it is in incremental redesign. You begin with a blank sheet of paper.
5—Implementing the new design	Different	Implementing an incremental redesign is easier since you are changing only elements of an existing process.	You are fundamentally changing the way the business operates. This requires a more radical implementation methodology.	In incremental redesign you still have to deal with change, but you deal with it on a much smaller scale. In fundamental redesign you are questioning and redesigning the very fiber of the organization. Its culture, its strategies, its measurement and reward systems—all will be affected.

| **How to use this section** | Even though a redesign project may seem to follow a linear path (i.e., from the intelligence stage to the design stage to the implementation stage), it does not. Implementation affects design, which affects how you clarify the request. As soon as you initiate the project you begin to affect its implementation. How you articulate your ideas and goals will be critical along each step of the way. Consequently, you should read through all of Section Two before starting. Furthermore, there are certain concepts and procedures described in later chapters that, depending on your unique circumstances, you may want to use much earlier in your redesign project. For example, Chapter 5 looks at barriers to process redesign. This is in Chapter 5 because if the barriers cannot be overcome the implementation of the redesign will fail. However, you could benefit from knowing about these barriers as you clarify the request (described in Chapter 2). |

How do you get involved?

The following scenarios highlight different ways in which you might become involved in a process redesign effort:

We need to develop products faster. Our cycle time is just horrible. Customers say we are the worst at introducing new products. I put together a team of individuals who will work with me to solve this problem. As we move forward on this project I know people will need to be trained, so I would like you to join this team.

We are not processing orders fast enough. Our on-time delivery is horrible. I think our people will need to know how to use the new order processing system. Could you take a look and let me know what you think?

The number of documents and forms around here is ridiculous. We've got to streamline and make them easier for people to use. Could you design a class to teach people how to fill out these forms?

In the next year we're going to automate and computerize a lot of our work. Given this, people will need to learn how to use the new system. We've got to teach them. I'd like you to join the team and give them your insight on how to teach people.

We've got to turn over our inventory more quickly. You know, I don't think our people know how to make this stuff move. You understand this "people stuff"—do you have time to join this team? I'd like your insights.

I'm sure you can think of many other such requests for help. Generally, you can categorize these requests into three areas: 1) a manager or executive asks you to join a cross-functional team; 2) a manager or executive seeks your help in addressing a particular performance issue; 3) you offer your services to a manager or executive.

Most fundamental redesign efforts involve a team of individuals. However, there may be some incremental redesign efforts that do not require a team, and you may be asked to do some preliminary analyses regarding a performance problem on your own.

How is this section organized?

To perform these activities:	Read this chapter:
• Define the organization's critical business issue • Determine who should sponsor the redesign • Determine who should guide the redesign • Optimize the redesign team • Determine how the team will work together • Create vehicles for communication	Chapter 2—Establishing Clear Goals for Process Redesign
• Understand the current culture • Understand the current financial system • Understand the current human resources system • Sketch the core process • Sketch or list the tasks that make up each activity in the process • Chart the flow of information • Chart the use of technology • Identify where activities occur • Add performance data • Determine current process success factors • Verify the process map • Prepare an executive summary report	Chapter 3—Understanding How the Current Process Works—and Doesn't Work

To perform these activities:	Read this chapter:
• Confirm the needs of the customer	Chapter 4—Creating the Simplest Possible Design to Solve the Business Problem
• Choose incremental or fundamental redesign	
• Identify the accomplishments and categorize the activities	
• Identify all performance gaps	
• Determine the root cause	
• Generate alternatives	
• Determine the best alternatives	
• Sketch the improved process	
• Confirm the objectives and effectiveness factors of the new design	
• Engage in breakthrough thinking	
• Create a general sketch of the new process	
• Determine how the current financial system needs to change to support the new design	
• Determine how the current human resources system needs to change to support the new design	
• Evaluate the new design	
• Design the organization chart	
• Prepare for executive and steering committee presentations	
• Create the implementation plan	Chapter 5—Overcoming Barriers to Implementation
• Overcome "real world" barriers	

CHAPTER 2

Establishing Clear Goals for Process Redesign

Purpose of this chapter

Process redesign involves looking at the activities that go into achieving a particular output—it involves looking at the "how." In each of the scenarios in the preceding introduction, there is some indication that how the work is done does not represent an optimal process. Developing new products is an example of a set of activities that may need improvement. A need to process orders more quickly could indicate that the way people currently perform this activity is no longer satisfactory. Requiring an unreasonable number of documents in order to achieve an output may indicate an excessive bureaucracy—the system generating the documents may need to be analyzed. Installing new information systems might change how work is done. As you can see, each of these problems could require a process redesign. Therefore, before you begin, you need to further clarify the request, to determine whether process redesign is really the right solution.

This chapter focuses on helping you clarify the organization's expectations, to clarify your charter. Managers are often unsure of what needs to be done and ask for help with analysis. Other times they know exactly the "solution" they want—without having probed for root causes—and only want implementation help. Both situations require you to ask for specifics. The focus in the beginning of any project is to come to a mutual understanding on the charter and the expectations. No matter how good your work, if it does not meet the sponsor's expectations you will not have achieved success.

How is this chapter organized?

To determine:	Follow this procedure:
What causes people to conclude there is a problem	Procedure 2.1—Define the Organization's Critical Business Issue
Who should ultimately be responsible	Procedure 2.2—Determine Who Should Sponsor the Redesign
Who needs to be involved to champion the process	Procedure 2.3—Determine Who Should Guide the Redesign
Who needs to be on the team	
The rules for how the team will function	Procedure 2.4—Optimize the Redesign Team
How to keep everyone empowered and "on board"	Procedure 2.5—Determine How the Team Will Work Together
	Procedure 2.6—Create Vehicles for Communication

Results

The outcomes this chapter aims for are 1) creating a clear charter, 2) understanding the critical business issue, 3) defining the metrics (data and specific parameters) used to indicate that an issue exists, and 4) securing the go-ahead to look at a specific current core process. In achieving these outcomes, you or your team may need to go through several rounds of data collection before the sponsor's request becomes clear.

If you follow the recommendations and procedures listed in this chapter, you should achieve the following results:

- A summary of the rationale for why the redesign is important.

- An agreement between the sponsor, steering committee, and redesign team regarding which cross-functional process will be redesigned.

- Clarification of the output or accomplishment desired. A clear, concise problem statement supported by clear metrics.

- Specific criteria on how to measure the success of the redesign effort (derived from the metrics in the problem statement).

- An understanding of how the organization and its customers are affected by this problem and the impact of closing the performance gap.

- A smoother implementation stage. A better understanding of people's concerns.

For More Information

Daniels, W. R. *Group Power I: A Manager's Guide to Using Task Force Meetings.* San Diego: Pfeiffer, 1986.

Daniels, W. R. *Group Power II: A Manager's Guide to Conducting Regular Meetings.* San Diego: Pfeiffer, 1990.

Davenport, T. H. *Process Innovation—Reengineering Work through Information Technology.* Boston, Mass.: Harvard Business School Press, 1993.

Eisenhardt, K. "Speed and Strategic Choice: How Managers Accelerate Decision Making." *California Management Review*, 1990, *32* (Spring), 39–54.

Hall, G., Rosenthal, J., and Wade, J. "How to Make Reengineering Really Work." *Harvard Business Review* (November–December 1993): 119–131.

Hammer, M. "Reengineering Work: Don't Automate, Obliterate." *Harvard Business Review* (July–August 1990): 104–112.

Hammer, M. and Champy, J. *Reengineering the Corporation.* New York: HarperCollins, 1993.

Kaplan, R. B. and Murdock, L. "Core Process Redesign." *McKinsey Quarterly*, 1991, *2*, 27–43.

Meyer, C. "How the Right Measures Help Teams Excel." *Harvard Business Review* (May–June 1994), *72* (3), 95–103.

Morris, D. and Brandon, J. *Reengineering Your Business.* New York: McGraw-Hill, 1993.

Pasmore, W. A. *Designing Effective Organizations—The Sociotechnical Systems Perspective.* New York: Wiley, 1988.

Rummler, G. A. and Brache, A. P. *Improving Performance.* San Francisco: Jossey-Bass, 1991.

Define the Organization's Critical Business Issue

Purpose of this procedure

There will be times when you will not have enough data to clearly and precisely define a critical business issue (performance gap). When this is the case, you must collect the appropriate data from the organization on the performance gap.

The purpose of this procedure is to determine the necessary scope of the proposed redesign effort. It will enable you to

- Specifically understand the business issue and the metrics used to alert management to its existence (i.e., inventory turns, sales from new products, and so on).

- Choose which core cross-functional process to redesign and determine its boundaries. It is important to choose the right process, so as to truly add value to the final output. Too often the process chosen is one that is narrowly defined within a particular function. The intent here is to define a cross-functional process and to choose the critical elements that will provide the customer with greater value.

- Develop a process vision that supports the business strategy.

The procedure often turns into a repetitive process: collect data, present to executive, collect more data, present to executive, clearly define business issue based on data, present to executive, recommend approach, agree on approach, begin redesign.

When to use this procedure

Use this procedure

- When an executive, possibly the sponsor, is in the initial stages of thinking about the issue.

- During your initial conversations with the team leader or sponsor, before the project begins.

- If you are asked to help select team members.

- When you have been asked to join a team.

Accomplishment   A tangible, measurable output.

Benchmark   An assessment of how other organizations have dealt with a similar issue.

Critical business issue   The business problem that the organization is trying to solve—the performance gap.

Core cross-functional process   The group of cross-functional activities that produces the output the customer wants. Most business can be broken down into five or six core processes (new product development, order fulfillment, customer service, materials procurement).

Problem   The gap between where the organization is today and where it would like to be tomorrow.

Process attributes   Characteristics the organization would like to see in the redesigned process (e.g., the entire process will be paperless).

Guidelines

Sometimes the critical business issue and the core process that should be redesigned to address the issue is not so clear. Work with the team and the initial sponsor to clearly define the issue, the boundaries (beginning and end points) of the core process you are considering redesigning, and whether redesigning this process will close the performance gap. Without boundaries you won't know where to start or end, how to define metrics, or how to measure success. In new product development, for example, the start may be a product concept and the end may be either a prototype released to a customer or a high-volume shipment.

A metric must be developed to determine how well a process functions. Usually this is done by measuring how the process performs today and then tailoring the metric as the process is changed. The easiest way to determine the appropriate metric to use is to ask others in the organization. Test and confirm what you hear from one executive with what you hear from others in the organization.

Before you start

1. Meet with the person making the initial request.

2. Confirm who should be interviewed to find out

   - The major outputs of the organization and where they go.

   - The major inputs and where they come from.

   - How the different functions (marketing, design, and so on) convert the input into the output, and how the output of one function is the input to another.

3. Confirm who will do the interviewing.

4. Confirm if there is any background information that needs to be assembled and studied.

5. Confirm who will be responsible for getting the information and studying it.

What to do

1. Gather data about the critical business issue through interviews and document searches. Stress these points:

   a) Evidence.

   - What are the specific results or outputs that are not being achieved?
   - How do you know there's a problem? Are you using any specific metrics that indicate this is a problem?
   - If this were not a problem, how would you know? By means of what indicators? How will you know when the problem is solved, specifically?

   b) Customer needs.

   - Who is the customer(s) for this output?
   - What does the customer say he or she wants? Why is this important to the customer?
   - What do you think the customer expects that has not been said? Why is this important to the customer?
   - What do you think would excite the customer? Why is this important to the customer?
   - Who is the customer's customer, and what do they need to be successful?

   c) Importance or severity of the problem.

   - Why is this output important to you?
   - What do you believe is the impact of closing this gap on customers and on the organization?
   - Is this critical business issue linked to the strategic plan? How?

2. Sketch the organizational systems affected by the critical business issue.

   - Include all the organizational systems affected by the critical business issue. Keep in mind 1) the major receiving systems, 2) the major output produced, and 3) the major inputs.

Steps	Suggested Questions & Approaches
3. Have the sponsor clearly define the boundaries (beginning and end points) of the relevant core process.	• In a new-product-development process, for example, the beginning might be the new product concept and the end might be the first prototype or high-volume production.
4. Determine 10–20 major activities in the core process.	• In the order-generation core process, for example, the major activities would be: 1) generate leads, 2) generate quotations, 3) enter order, 4) fill order, 5) send invoice.
5. Challenge whether this is truly the best process to redesign.	• Is this the best process to redesign to address the critical business issue? • Will this redesign have an impact on our customers?
6. Ask if the redesign is feasible.	• Can this process be redesigned?
7. Ask about potential effects on the organization.	• Will redesigning this process affect overall unit performance? How? • In redesigning this process to close the performance gap, will we need to redesign incrementally or fundamentally?
8. Confirm the choice with the team's initial sponsor.	• Meet with him or her and ask if you are on the right track (that is, does he or she agree that redesigning this particular core process will improve business performance and address the critical business issue?).
9. Give the process a name.	• For example, a process might be called new product development or concept to prototype; or order fulfillment or order to ship.

Example

Often the core process requiring redesign will be indicated in your conversation with the initial sponsor about the critical business issue. For example, the person might say, "Our delivery times stink! We only deliver on time 60 percent of the time, and our customers can't get what they want when they want it. We've got to make it better or we're in big trouble!" This would seem to indicate a problem with the order fulfillment process.

Once you've identified a possible process problem, you need to consider the system as a whole. Consider the example of a welding supply business. The following is a rough diagram of such an organization. Notice how items flow into the system and then out to customers.

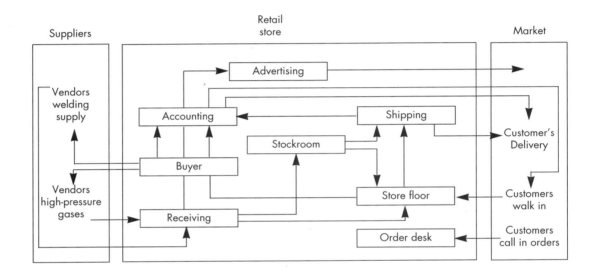

Order fulfillment

Within the total system there are various core processes that describe the organization's activities. Notice that the core processes are cross-functional; they cut across the organization horizontally. Some organizations can describe everything they do in terms of only five or six core processes. The following diagram depicts a typical order fulfillment process at a macro level. This order fulfillment process begins with the customer placing an order and ends with the customer being billed. The beginning and ending points of the process give you some idea of the boundaries within which you are working.

Determine Who Should Sponsor the Redesign

Purpose of this procedure

The purpose of this procedure is to clarify the sponsor. The sponsor or leader of the entire redesign effort is a critical element in the success of the project. The sponsor must have the authority to alter the organizational structure, managers' roles and responsibilities, and any other variable that may affect how people work. The sponsor should be an executive who is high enough in the organization to 1) have authority over the entire process, beginning to end; 2) have the authority to change support systems (reward systems, measurement systems, organizational structures, and so on); 3) be able to devote 20 to 60 percent of his or her time to the effort (60 percent during implementation). In most cases the sponsor is the CEO or other top manager in the business. The sponsor will work closely with a steering committee and the redesign team.

When to use this procedure

Use this procedure

- When an executive, possibly the sponsor, is in the initial stages of thinking about the issue.

- During your initial conversations with the team leader or sponsor, before the project begins.

- When you have been asked to join a team.

Terms you may not know

Charter   A contract or a concrete understanding between the sponsor and the redesign team specifying what the team will try to accomplish and by what time—the goal.

Sponsor   The top executive who is leading the overall change effort. The person who will remove resource roadblocks and who has the authority to change anything related to the process being redesigned.

Team leader   The leader and manager of the redesign team.

Guidelines

The following table details guidelines for identifying the sponsor.

If...	Then...
The charter of the team specifies a major improvement in organizational performance, such as to decrease overall business costs by 25%, reduce new product development time by a factor of 10, or increase inventory turns by a factor of 3 . . .	The top executive needs to be intimately involved with the effort; he or she might be the team leader, and should definitely be the sponsor.
You believe that the project will affect how certain functions operate, such as human resources, finance, information systems; or you think it will affect the organizational culture, reward systems, measuring systems, and so on . . .	The top executive needs to be intimately involved with the effort; he or she should be the sponsor.
The project will not affect the entire business, does not cross functions, or will not involve redesigning a core business process . . .	The top executive may need only to be aware of the effort.
The process you are looking at crosses several functions . . .	The sponsor of the project should be the person who has formal authority over all the functions.

What to do

Steps	Suggested Questions & Approaches
1. Discuss the request with the team leader. Meet with the team and the team leader to confirm what is expected and by whom.	• What is the charter of this effort? • What are we trying to accomplish and by when? • Who has chartered this team? • Who are the other people guiding this effort?
2. Have the team suggest a sponsor who meets the criteria stated in the guidelines.	
3. Meet with a person who has adequate authority and ask what he or she thinks about this effort.	In fundamental redesign the top executive must participate actively. The organization will be watching his or her behaviors. He or she must believe that fundamental redesign is necessary.
4. Determine if there is a way to get his or her support (publicly).	You may need to collect some preliminary performance data and then ask the top executive for support.
5. Once you have his or her commitment, explain to the executive what it takes to redesign a process and how this redesigned process will affect the performance of the business.	Manage expectations carefully. In most redesign efforts there is an initial dip in performance as the organization makes the transition to its new state. Make the executive aware of this possibility and work with him or her to minimize the effect.

Determine Who Should Guide the Redesign

Purpose of this procedure

A steering committee guides the overall change effort. The optimal steering committee is composed of individuals from different departments or functions and different levels within the organization. This is the body that will guide the sponsor, the executive team, and the redesign team and provide recommendations. The redesign team will bring its findings and recommendations back to this steering committee for review.

When to use this procedure

Use this procedure

- When an executive, possibly the sponsor, is in the initial stages of thinking about the issue.
- When the project looks like it will become a fundamental redesign effort that will affect the entire business.
- During your initial conversations with the team leader or sponsor, before the project begins.
- When you have been asked to join a team.

Terms you may not know

Steering committee   A committee of executives, managers, and individual contributors from various departments or functions who will advise the sponsor, the executive team, and the redesign team.

Before you start

1. Confirm whether or not a steering committee already exists.
2. If yes, determine how many people are on the committee, who they are, and their level in the organization.
3. If no, have the team generate an initial list of people as possible candidates and state why they think they should be on the committee.

What to do

Steps	Suggested Questions & Approaches
1. If you have the opportunity to give input to the sponsor before the steering committee is created:	
a) Recommend people who can look at the entire business.	The trick in creating a committee is to balance your need for authority and commitment of senior executives with your need for the knowledge of day-to-day operations and commitment of people further down in the organization. Furthermore, the committee should stay at a manageable size (less than fifteen).
b) Recommend people who can influence others.	Look at a diagonal slice of the organization (multiple levels and multiple functions).
	Choose the organization's best performers to be on the committee.
	Choose executives that have a large stake in the change effort.
	Choose individuals that are highly respected by their peers. There are usually some individuals in the organization who have enhanced influence and power simply because they are respected by others.
	Suggest that the sponsor be the formal leader of the committee.
2. If a committee already exists, add members according to the above criteria.	Steering committees should never contain only executives. This tells the people in the organization that this is a "management thing."

Procedure 2.4	## *Optimize the Redesign Team*

Purpose of this procedure

The people on the redesign team are also an important element in the success of the effort. The importance of a "balanced" team cannot be over-emphasized. This means that there should not be ten manufacturing engineers redesigning a new-product-introduction process, for example. It means you should have people on the team who truly know how the work gets done. This implies that redesign is not to be done solely by a group of senior managers.

When to use this procedure

Use this procedure

- When an executive, possibly the sponsor, is in the initial stages of thinking about the issue.
- During your initial conversations with the team leader or sponsor, before the project begins.
- If you are asked to help select team members.
- When you have been asked to join a team.

Terms you may not know

Redesign team   The group of individuals that will analyze the current process, make recommendations for improvement, and help implement a redesigned process.

Before you start

1. Find out if a team exists and who is on it.
2. Confirm what skills, knowledge, and organizational support the team members bring to the effort.

What to do

1. If you have the opportunity to give input to the sponsor before the team is created, suggest criteria for selecting team members. Create a small team (preferably not more than ten people).

The team should include members who

- Come from the departments or functions involved in the process.

- Are the organization's best performers.

- Have specialized expertise such as information systems, problem solving/redesign, or marketing experience.

- Know the process.

- Don't know the process.

- Are highly respected in the organization and are able to work around the rules. This is especially important for the team leader.

- Have complementary skills. You need individuals with technical, functional, and interpersonal skills.

- Are customers, internal or external.

- Can devote a significant portion of their time to the redesign effort.

(continued on next page)

Steps	Suggested Questions & Approaches
2. Confirm that they will have the time.	A fundamental redesign team should work full-time, at least through the design phase. Fundamental redesign is not just another project that can be put on someone's already full plate.
	A full-time team working on a clearly defined project plan will help keep the effort from becoming an exercise in analysis. This is often a major concern with executives. A full-time team can accelerate the analysis portion of the project.
	If you cannot get a full-time team and the top manager or CEO is not the person sponsoring the effort, you should *not* begin a fundamental redesign project. The effort is too great and the risk is too high. Without this critical variable in place it will most likely fail.
3. If a team already exists, confirm that the team is small and cross-functional and meets most of the criteria mentioned above.	If the team is *too* small (three or four individuals), you can ask the sponsor if others can join the team.
	If the team contains seven to nine people but it does not appear cross-functional, you can suggest that certain experts (i.e., Information Systems, Finance) are brought in on an ad hoc basis to give their input.
	If the team is not staffed correctly, you can suggest that the team should be re-chartered with new members.

Example　　　　ABC Corporation wants to embark on a fundamental redesign effort. Only 20 percent of the organization's year-to-date sales came from products developed in the last three years. The organization has compiled data that indicates that it takes anywhere from one year to five years to introduce a new product. Their vision is to cut the time it takes to introduce new products in half and to increase sales from new products to 60 percent.

Due to converging technologies many new competitors are entering the market with similar or substitute products. It is clear that the long-term position of the company in several key markets is at stake.

One of the senior executives puts together a team of seven core individuals who will devote 100 percent of their time to the effort. These consist of Manufacturing, Information Systems, Operations, Marketing, Engineering, and Human Resources. In addition, there are three additional people who will devote 50 percent of their time to the effort. These people are from Finance and Quality. The team will expand charter subteams and grow depending on the demands of each stage in the redesign project. The senior executive will devote 20 percent of his time to the effort for the first six months and 50 percent of his time during its implementation. The team will focus on the new-product-development process, starting with new product concept and ending with high-volume shipments.

Procedure 2.5	# *Determine How the Team Will Work Together*

Purpose of this procedure

The team needs to have one methodology that it will follow, and every team member and committee member must understand the approach the team is going to take.

The redesign group also needs to develop skills on how to interact as a team. The group will at times experience conflict and disagreement, and it needs to have the skills necessary to work through such conflict.

When to use this procedure

Use this procedure when you have been asked to join a team.

Terms you may not know

Common framework The model that everyone on the team should be working with.

Before you start

1. Confirm that the team has already been trained in process redesign and teamwork.

2. Find out what resources are available to help the team learn more about process redesign and teamwork.

What to do

Steps	Suggested Questions & Approaches
1. Develop a common framework.	Use this book as the vehicle to create that framework.
	Another approach is to send the entire team to a workshop on process redesign so that everyone on the team understands what it takes to truly redesign a cross-functional process.
2. Clarify the basic group process.	Use a good book. Have the entire team read the same book, and then follow the advice given. There are many good books on how to lead meetings and how to lead groups. The best I've found are two by William Daniels (see reference list).
	Ask a professional facilitator, either internal or external, to help your team with the first couple of meetings. Make it clear to the facilitator that your intent is not to use him or her all the time, but only to help your group get started.

Create Vehicles for Communication

Purpose of this procedure

The purpose of this procedure is to begin to create a communication plan to make it clear to the rest of the organization what the redesign team is working on. Compile a redesign position paper, pulling together everything your team has learned so far into a "reason for redesign" paper or presentation. The scope and circulation of your position paper will depend on the magnitude of change the redesign requires. Sharing the redesign position paper begins the process of openly communicating what the organization is trying to do, and it links the redesign effort to the organization's overall strategic plan, initiatives, and so on. The outcome of this procedure is the beginning of a shared reality—and understanding of why we are redesigning.

People need to understand why the organization is redesigning a process; they need to know it is not just another program or fad. People need to see that there is no other alternative to redesign if the organization wants to meet its strategic objectives. The position paper should answer the questions Why, So what, and Why should I care.

As people hear about the redesign effort and its potential impact, there will be some concern. The key is to let people know what is happening. It is often the ambiguity surrounding change that makes people uncomfortable and resistant. Unfortunately, too often top management thinks redesign efforts should proceed in secret because of the unrest they will cause. But keeping the effort secret causes even greater unrest.

When to use this procedure

Use this procedure when you suspect that fundamental redesign will be necessary. If you are planning to redesign incrementally, you will probably not need an extensive position paper, but a communication plan will still be helpful.

Terms you may not know

Communication plan   All the steps necessary for the redesign team to ensure that the entire organization has a good understanding of the effort.

Disagree and commit   An operating principle that mirrors business reality. In many cases people will move forward to get something accomplished although they may not totally agree with decisions. They can, however, commit to the decision. Insisting on consensus in today's competitive business environment is often an example of wishful thinking, and people recognize this fact.

Paradigm   A model (operating under today's paradigm equals operating under today's model).

Redesign position paper   A formal explanation of why the organization must redesign.

Guidelines

1. Distribute the position paper as widely as possible. The more people who understand the reasons for redesign and the critical business issue in question, the better.

2. The paper should be in summary form and it should not be longer than ten pages.

3. The intent of your communication efforts should be to uncover disagreements and gain commitment as much as is possible. In some cases people will not agree with the stated need or the methodology. Some people will be resistant because it may change the power structure. In cases where there is disagreement over rationale for redesigning, it is good to have a strong and respected sponsor and team leader.

4. When presenting or collecting data, always tell people what you intend to do with the information.

5. Operate within the "disagree and commit" paradigm. There are many situations where people do not agree for a variety of reasons but they are willing to commit themselves to support the effort. They may disagree with your methodology or the priority of the critical business issue you define, but they will commit themselves to helping you redesign the process. In many cases, if you are direct and straightforward and do not expect or require agreement, people will commit to helping you even though they disagree with you. They understand that in business there will always be plans with which they disagree, but they also want to get things going and get things done.

What to do

Steps	Suggested Questions & Approaches
1. Pull together all of the information gathered so far and write a draft paper or create a draft presentation.	Once all the information is collected, one team member should create a draft of the paper and then present it to the redesign team. The redesign team should critique and edit the paper.
2. Discuss the paper with the sponsor. Describe the purpose and find out how widely the position paper should be distributed.	Get the sponsor's input and an initial list of people to whom the document should be sent for additional critiques. Your sponsor will know how to approach certain people for this purpose. Your sponsor will know whether the redesign project can go forward despite a particular person's disagreeing. He or she will know whether someone needs to talk with that person.
3. Send the paper to a selected audience and schedule a short meeting. Ask these questions:	• Is there anything in this paper that does not make sense to you? • Do you agree with the basic premise and rationale as stated? • Do we need to modify anything?
4. Summarize the input from the meeting and discuss your next steps.	

Steps	Suggested Questions & Approaches
5. Identify ways to communicate the team's progress.	Brainstorm all the ways people in the organization currently receive information in general, and how they could receive information about the redesign project specifically.
	If possible, meet with a communication expert, either internal or external. Hiring a communication consultant to help you develop a communication methodology may be worth the money. Keeping the organization informed is one of the most critical elements of any redesign project.
6. Develop a communication plan.	Communication is two-way. The team needs to determine how the organization's members can communicate with the redesign team.
	Assign one member of the redesign team—with the help of a senior executive—the responsibility of communicating progress to the organization and maintaining the continuous flow of information to people throughout the redesign process.
	Think of having small, informal meetings with people throughout the organization to get their ongoing input on the process.
7. Determine how the redesign position paper best fits into the communication plan.	The paper may be only the first piece of the communication plan; you might also publish subsequent, follow-up papers so the organization can read about what is happening.

Example

Here's a possible table of contents for a redesign paper:

I.   The Critical Business Issue and How It Affects Our Competitiveness (Why We Have to Do This).

II.   How We Intend to Address This—The Core Process That Will Be Redesigned

III. Process Vision and Objectives

IV. Who Will Redesign and Why We All Need to Work on This

V.   The Redesign Methodology—The Project Plan

VI. How We Intend to Keep People Informed—The Communication Plan

The following is an excerpt from a top management communications meeting that highlights the scope of a fundamental redesign project:

This change effort will affect all functions, from marketing to engineering to manufacturing. Our entire organization will be affected and we anticipate this project taking two years. Realize that this project is highly visible and will affect all of us in profound ways. We will need to develop new skills and capabilities. In other words, what we are embarking on today is huge.

The redesign team has been formed and consists of representatives from all functions. All of their meetings are open-door, and anyone can attend. Furthermore, they have decided to publish a paper, as well as an electronic newsletter, that talks about the effort. This paper, called the White Paper, is available electronically in the Process Redesign Folder on the Quality Server. It is also available by calling my secretary at extension 4444. We will be having quarterly communications meetings focused exclusively on this effort, during which myself and my entire staff will be open to questions. The team is working on a position paper on why this redesign is necessary and a project plan that, when completed, will be posted. I've covered many of the reasons why we need to do this today, but if you want more detailed information take a look at the White Paper. Anyone concerned with this project or who has questions can also come see me or my staff anytime. I will be working closely with the redesign team on this project so that I can better understand what happens around here day to day.

I realize that this has been just a brief overview, but I would like to open it for questions at this point.

CHAPTER 3

Understanding How the Current Process Works—and Doesn't Work

Purpose of this chapter

At this point you have clarified the request from the sponsor, you understand the importance of the critical business issue, you have agreed on what core process to redesign, and you have the steering committee's and sponsor's commitment to move forward with the project.

You can now move into the "creating the current picture" phase of redesign, in which you try to understand the current system and the current core process. Do not attempt to close the performance gap yet. First you need to develop a thorough understanding of the gap and the possible causes for it.

Before you can change anything, you need to understand how the organization operates today. This chapter focuses on the information you need to collect in order to successfully model the current business operations. *The goal is to capture how work flows through the system.*

For any given process you want to determine the following points (illustrated here with the example of a typical insurance company's business operations):

- The major accomplishments or major outputs. (In an insurance underwriting process, a major accomplishment is a "go/no go" decision on whether or not to underwrite someone.)

- The relationship of the process outputs to customers and suppliers. (Customers want a quick decision on whether or not the company will underwrite.)

- The major activities that are currently needed to achieve a particular accomplishment. (For an underwriting decision, the major activities are to check actuarial tables, check profiles of industries, do a Dun and Bradstreet analysis, and so on.)

- The information and technology used (and how they are used) in performing each of these activities. (Insurance companies use published hardcover copies of actuarial tables.)

- The length of time it takes to perform each activity. (It takes two days to check insurance industry profiles.) Be sure to capture the difference between ostensible process times (e.g., it takes thirty seconds to process an invoice) versus actual cycle times (e.g., the invoice is dropped in a box, looked over by John, sent to Sally to sign, and so on, and it takes two days to achieve the accomplishment).

- The cost of each activity. (It costs an insurance company three hundred dollars to check industry profiles.)

- The people currently responsible for achieving each output or performing certain sets of activities.

- The performance metrics currently used (how do you know if an output is accomplished, when it is accomplished, and how well it is accomplished). (For example, once an underwriting decision is made, a letter is sent to the applicant. It takes ten days from receipt of an application to sending of the letter.)

This chapter provides you with a roadmap for gathering and assembling the data you will need. There are two critical questions you should always keep in mind when gathering data:

1. How much data do you need to create a shared understanding of the current problem or opportunity? The data must adequately describe the current cross-functional process and the context in which it operates.

2. How much data do you need to help people understand the necessity for redesign? Careful documentation of the need for the project will help make the implementation of the new process as easy and seamless as possible.

How is this chapter organized?

To determine:	Follow this procedure:
What behaviors are currently valued and rewarded	Procedure 3.1—Understand the Current Culture
How the financial system reinforces current behaviors	Procedure 3.2—Understand the Current Financial System
How Human Resource priorities reinforce current behaviors	Procedure 3.3—Understand the Current Human Resources Systems
What the process looks like	Procedure 3.4—Sketch the Core Process
All the things that happen over the course of the process	Procedure 3.5—Sketch or List the Tasks That Make Up Each Activity
Where people get the information they need, and what they do with it	Procedure 3.6—Chart the Flow of Information
What people use to do their job	Procedure 3.7—Chart the Use of Technology
How spread apart people are	Procedure 3.8—Identify Where Activities Occur
Where time and costs add up	Procedure 3.9—Add Performance Data
What could be used to measure success	Procedure 3.10—Determine Current Process Success Factors
Whether what you have learned is accurate	Procedure 3.11—Verify the Process Map
How to present your findings	Procedure 3.12—Prepare an Executive Summary Report

Guidelines

There are many different types of tools you can use to model both the overall business operation and a specific core cross-functional process. Flowcharts are the most popular and widely used tool for providing a basic understanding of how work flows through an organizational system. Given the wide use of flowcharting, this book uses flowcharts as the basic tool to understanding work. There are many good flowcharting software packages available. Other available tools include tree diagrams, fishbone diagrams, Warnier-Orr diagrams, network models, and so on (Morris and Brandon, 1993).

Software

You can also use project management software. Even though project management software is not intended as a business process modeling tool, it makes looking at activities more efficient since you can use the computer to capture the data. This type of software uses the same building blocks as flowcharts (inputs, activities, outputs), and it also allows you to add data on resources, times, costs, and such directly into your computer. This gives you the ability to create some basic reports, summaries, and overviews.

Another approach is to use activity-based software tools that have recently been developed, given the popularity of business process redesign. I have found these tools highly effective and efficient. They allow managers and consultants to model complex business processes quickly and easily. They are much more sophisticated in modeling processes within a dynamic environment than flowcharts or project management software and should be used in conjunction with one of these other tools. These activity-based software tools allow you to capture the complexity of a cross-functional process, the multiple variations of a process, and the specific data regarding costs, resources, times, and such. This gives you the ability to create sophisticated reports, summaries, and overviews quickly and efficiently.

The best activity-based software tool I have found is Workflow BPR by Virtual Management, Inc. This tool is capable of realistically modeling the work that people perform and graphically capturing all of the variations of a business process. The tool provides metrics on work responsibility, costing, financial accounting, time, and such. Tables and graphs are easily generated, sorted and analyzed.

Results   If you follow the recommendations and procedures listed in this chapter, you should achieve an accurate model of how the organization's core cross-functional process operates. This model will help you as you enter the design phase of the project. Perhaps more importantly, it will help you give management a better understanding of how the organization operates and the need for redesign, which will prove invaluable when you reach the implementation stage of the project.

Chapter organization   The following information-gathering steps are described sequentially; however, do not think of them in a linear fashion. For example, I have written first about charting activities, then about charting information, and then about charting time; but as you collect data you may learn about how long something takes in the process of learning about the information needed for a particular accomplishment.

For More Information

Beer, M., Eisenstat, R. A., and Spector, B. "Why Change Programs Don't Produce Change." *Harvard Business Review* (November–December 1990): 158–166.

Beer, S. *Diagnosing the System for Organizations.* New York: Wiley, 1985.

Davenport, T. H. *Process Innovation—Reengineering Work through Information Technology.* Boston, Mass.: Harvard Business School Press, 1993.

Eisenhardt, K. "Speed and Strategic Choice: How Managers Accelerate Decision Making." *California Management Review*, 1990, *32* (Spring), 39–54.

El Sawy, O. A. and Khorshid, H. S. *A Design Theory of Virtual Workflows.* Research Paper IOM 94–13. University of Southern California, July, 1994.

Galbraith, J. R. *Organization Design.* Reading, Mass.: Addison-Wesley, 1977.

Hammer, M. "Reengineering Work: Don't Automate, Obliterate." *Harvard Business Review* (July–August 1990): 104–112.

Hammer, M., and Champy, J. *Reengineering the Corporation.* New York: HarperCollins, 1993.

Harrison, R. "Understanding Your Organization's Character." *Harvard Business Review* (May–June 1972), 119–128.

Jaques, E. *Requisite Organization.* Arlington, Va.: Cason Hall, 1989.

Kaplan, R. B., and Murdock, L. (1991). "Core Process Redesign." *McKinsey Quarterly*, 1991, *2*, 27–43.

Leeds, D. "The Art of Asking Questions." *Training and Development* (January 1993): 57–62.

Lincoln, Y. S., and Guba, E. G. *Naturalistic Inquiry.* Newbury Park, Calif.: Sage Publications, 1985.

Mackenzie, K. D. "The Process Approach to Organizational Design." *Human Systems Management*, 1989, *8*, 31–43.

Miller, J. *Living Systems.* New York: McGraw-Hill, 1978.

Mintzberg, H. *Mintzberg on Management.* New York: Free Press, 1989.

Morris, D., and Brandon, J. *Reengineering Your Business.* New York: McGraw-Hill, 1993.

Pasmore, W. A. *Designing Effective Organizations—The Sociotechnical Systems Perspective.* New York: Wiley, 1988.

Perrow, C. *Organizational Analysis.* Belmont, Calif.: Wadsworth, 1990.

Porras, J. I. *Stream Analysis: A Powerful Way to Diagnose and Manage Organization Change.* Reading, Mass.: Addison-Wesley, 1987.

Rummler, G. A., and Brache, A. P. *Improving Performance.* San Francisco: Jossey-Bass, 1991.

Schaffer, R. H., and Thomson, H. A. "Successful Change Programs Begin with Results." *Harvard Business Review* (January–February 1992): 80–89.

Shapiro, B. P., Rangan, V. K., and Sviokla, J. J. "Staple Yourself to an Order." *Harvard Business Review* (July–August 1992): 113–122.

Spadaford, J. F. "Reengineering Commercial Loan Servicing at First Chicago." *National Productivity Review* (Winter 1992–93), 65–72.

Tomasko, R. M. *Rethinking the Corporation: The Architecture of Change.* New York: AMACOM, 1993.

Turney, P. *Common Cents.* Hillsboro, Ore.: Cost Technology, 1992.

Weinberg, G. M. *Rethinking Systems Analysis and Design.* Boston: Little, Brown, 1982.

Purpose of this procedure

The purpose of this procedure is to help you better understand the organizational culture. This will be important when you are determining how best to implement the redesign project.

When to use this procedure

Use this procedure

- If the redesign team feels that the organization is resistant to change.
- If the team thinks that some managers do not recognize the need for change.
- If the team thinks it needs to better understand the values and beliefs the organization holds, before it begins to redesign.
- If the executive staff is unclear on how people feel and think about the organization, or if they think everything is fine but the team thinks there are serious issues to be addressed.
- When people in the organization make comments about bureaucracy, lack of trust, lack of accountability, lack of fun, and so on.

Terms you may not know

Artifacts   The visible, tangible representations of an organization's culture (e.g., closed offices versus cubicles).

Assumptions   The underlying principles that guide an organization's behavior.

Organizational culture   The assumptions, artifacts, and values and beliefs present in an organization.

Values and beliefs   What the organization holds in high regard, based on its assumptions.

Guidelines

To understand an organization's culture, look at these three levels:

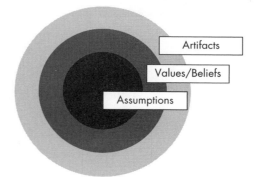

To understand a culture you need to uncover the assumptions at its core. For example, does the organization place a higher value on achievement or on ascription? Achievement refers to what one accomplishes (performance), while ascription pertains to who one is (academic degree held, experience, age, and so on). For example, if the organization operates under the ascriptive assumption it values seniority. People with more seniority are seen as better performers. Therefore it can be seen that an organization's values and beliefs directly depend upon its core assumptions. And the artifacts of the organization's culture are the visible, tangible representations of those values and beliefs (e.g., higher pay based on seniority only, not on performance).

Before you start

1. Clearly define what you are trying to accomplish with the survey

2. Find out if the organization has already done a survey, and if it captured the data that you need.

3. If the team needs to do a survey, have them decide who they want to survey and how they want to conduct the survey (use a printed questionnaire, conduct personal interviews, and so on).

4. Find out what organization resources the team may use in conducting the survey.

5. Confirm how the survey's subjects will be selected.

6. Confirm who will distribute the survey, conduct the interviews, summarize the data, and so on.

7. Determine how the results will be shared and with whom.

What to do

Steps	Suggested Questions & Approaches
1. Conduct surveys and/or interviews.	
Find out what groups hold which beliefs.	Determine how widely beliefs are shared across populations (departments and levels).
	Determine what beliefs are unique to specific populations.
Find out how willing people are to change or to consider new ideas.	How open are people to new ideas?
	How much analysis is expected before management will champion a new idea?
	Are there certain critical variables that will convince people that change is necessary more than other variables?
Find out how people feel about risk.	Determine the culture's risk tolerance.
	Determine how conservative the culture is, fiscally and otherwise.
	Ask if radically new ideas have ever been introduced in the past. If so, how?
	Determine the culture's basic assumptions regarding risk, change, analysis, safety, and openness.
Find out who and what is celebrated.	Who are the organization's heroes? What makes them heroes (fostering change, encouraging innovation, taking risks, etc.)?
	Is innovation celebrated?
	What are the rites and rituals reinforcing conformity?

Steps	Suggested Questions & Approaches
Find out what is valued.	Who gets promoted?
	To get ahead, is it more important to be political and posturing or to do what is best for the business and its customers?
	How much time is spent doing activities for their own sake rather than for achieving results?
	Are people measured on results or on completing many activities?
	Are people driven by *obtaining* results or by *looking like* they're obtaining results?
	Is it easy to get things accomplished, or is there too much bureaucracy?
Find out what the level of trust is.	What percentage of your decisions do not need approval or a signature from someone else?
	How candid can you be about issues?
	What has happened to people who have been direct, open, and completely honest about issues?
2. Summarize the data.	If a standardized instrument was used, the instrument usually cites guidelines for interpreting the data. If the team created its own questions, use someone qualified in data analysis.
3. Share the results.	Before you conducted the survey, you should have clearly defined what you were trying to accomplish and with whom you would share the results.

Example

A redesign team discovers the following about their organization's culture:

- It can be "career limiting" to openly challenge ideas.
- Activities are more important than results.
- Doing "the right thing" is more important than doing things right.
- Managers control only 60 percent of their budgets, yet they get evaluated on 100 percent of budget item outputs.

The team concludes that there is little trust in the organization and that the wrong behaviors are rewarded. It shares this information in its data summary with executives, stressing the point that the newly designed process must support and reward accomplishment.

Understand the Current Financial System

Purpose of this procedure

The purpose of this procedure is to determine what the organization's financial practices are, how the redesign project will affect its financial system, and what specific elements in the financial system must change in order for the newly designed process to work.

It is essential that you accurately determine how the organization measures costs. Cost is a critical variable in business, since managers are rewarded or punished depending on financial performance. How these numbers are decided drives certain behaviors within the organization. Since much of the human behavior in the organization is driven by the profit and loss (P&L) statement, it is important to understand the organization's financial metrics.

When to use this procedure

Use this procedure when you need to understand how an organization's accounting practices and financial measurement conventions drive its behavior.

Terms you may not know

Allocation   How an organization spreads its costs across its various departments, functions, and so on.

Cost accounting   The branch of accounting that deals primarily with business costs.

Cost plus   A process by which an organization determines how much a product costs, and then adds on an amount for profit.

Margin   The difference between revenue and cost, measured at various places on the income statement (e.g., the manufacturing margin can be calculated as the difference between revenue from sales and manufacturing cost).

Performance management plan   An individual's goals.

Target costing   A process by which an organization determines how much a product can sell for in the market and then works backward to come up with a cost low enough to produce a profit.

Before you start

1. Meet with the redesign team to determine what performance management information (e.g., goals) it already has and what it still needs.

2. Determine how the team will get what it needs and who on the team will do it.

3. Determine who else in the organization needs to be involved.

What to do

Steps	Suggested Questions & Approaches
1. Collect performance management plans.	Determine the goals of each of the executives involved in the core process, if they have goals. Depending on the process, this may involve questioning all functional heads.
2. Compare the organization's financial rewards and what it tracks with what has been identified as the critical business issue.	Look for whether financial rewards and the metrics that determine them support closing the performance gap. For example, if the critical issue is customer deliveries and deliveries are tracked but senior management is only rewarded for lower costs, the rewards work against closing the gap.
Ask questions specific to the business issue.	If new product introductions is an issue, does the organization use metrics regarding the cost of delay? Do managers know how much revenue is lost by introducing a product one week late?
3. Interview executives and managers.	Ask managers what gets talked about from a financial point of view during operations reviews. Use the data already collected as a guide to the discussion.
Ask what financial information managers have.	• What financial metrics does the organization track? What metrics are important? • How does the organization determine prices for products or services? • What can you tell me about the cost accounting system? • How are costs determined? • Does this organization use target costing or a cost-plus methodology?

Steps	Suggested Questions & Approaches
Ask if the financial system gives managers good data.	• If I wanted to know how much certain activities cost, how would I find this information?
	• Do we know which activities add value, which do not add value, and how much these respective activities cost?
	• How important is performance to budget?
	• How are budgets set (by department, by function, etc.)?
	• By what process are budgets set?
	• How are budgets allocated?
	• What is the budget cycle? When is next year's budget determined?
Ask what the score card is.	• How is success determined based on these financial metrics?
	• What does the CEO or general manager emphasize from a financial standpoint?
4. Summarize what you learned about the current financial systems.	• Clearly state how the financial metrics reinforce certain behaviors.

Example

A redesign team discovers that

- The people in a company do not know what it costs if a product is delivered two weeks late (they do not know the cost of delay in the new-product-introduction process).

- They do know what percentage of the company's sales come from various different products and how old those products are (e.g., 50 percent of sales are from products introduced in the last two years).

- They do not know what it costs to process one order.

- They do know how much revenue is generated by some products and how profitable those products are.

The team decides they still need to find out exactly what certain costs are (cost of delay, cost of processing orders, and so on). They conclude that the newly designed process must generate better financial data than the current system does.

Understand the Current Human Resources Systems

Purpose of this procedure

The purpose of this procedure is to help you identify the human resources (HR) systems that might affect your redesign effort. The HR department may place strict guidelines on what you can and cannot do. When you embark on a redesign effort, jobs change, the way information is distributed changes, and the way you manage resources (human and other) changes. The magnitude of this change depends on whether you improve processes incrementally or fundamentally. In either case, however, human resources will be affected.

When to use this procedure

Use this procedure when you need to understand how human resource systems drive behavior.

Before you start

1. Meet with the redesign team to determine what performance management information it already has and what it still needs.

2. Determine how the team will get what it needs and who on the team will do it.

3. Determine who else in the organization needs to be involved.

What to do

Steps	Suggested Questions & Approaches
1. Have the team identify who to interview in order to find out how the current performance management system works. Ask about what gets rewarded.	Collect the performance reviews of each executive involved in the core process. Depending on the process, this may include all functional heads. • What do you think of the current system of measuring performance? • What are you rewarded for, informally and formally? • What are other people rewarded for, informally and formally? • What gets rewarded in this organization? What gets punished? Why is that?
Ask about performance evaluations.	• How is performance measured? Formally? Informally? • How often is performance formally evaluated? • Are certain items in your evaluations weighted more heavily than others? Are some more important?
Ask how valuable the evaluation (performance management) process is.	• Is your performance the critical variable in evaluation, or is who you know, how you act, and how well you play the game more critical? • What is important to you? To your boss? • How does the performance management system reinforce your business objectives? How does it work against your objectives? • Which of your current goals relate to this evaluation process? Is there alignment or conflict between the goals for the process being redesigned and what you are evaluated on?

Steps	Suggested Questions & Approaches
2. Identify how the current compensation system works. Ask about the basis for bonuses and raises.	• Does the company have a bonus or incentive system for its executives? • What are bonuses or incentives based on? What are the specific metrics? • How are these rewards linked to the core process in question? • What in your opinion needs to change in the rewards system to better reinforce the improvement of this core process? • How are people paid? Are there incentives? • How are raises determined? What is the process? • What are managers rewarded for? • Is there a bonus program in which everyone participates? What is this based on?

(continued on next page)

Steps	Suggested Questions & Approaches
3. Identify how the current training system works. Ask about who gets trained and how.	• How would you rate the quality and timeliness of training in this company? • What do you think needs to happen from a training standpoint to support the type of change proposed? • What is training doing well, and where could it improve? • Do you have focused training? Are there certain training courses that all managers must take (so they'll all have a common framework) or can managers take whatever they want? • Does training take a performance technology approach focusing on improving on the job performance? • What needs to change, if anything, in training to keep the business competitive? Imagine that everything had to function ten to twenty times faster—what would have to change to make this possible? • How is the decision made to offer training?

Steps	Suggested Questions & Approaches
4. Identify the overall work force skills. Ask about the skill level of people in general.	• What is your sense of the skill level of the work force? Where do you see skill deficiencies? How are they currently being addressed? Feel free to break your response into any categories you want (managers, operators, etc.).
	• If we needed to develop products ten times faster, what basic skills would people need to have?
5. Identify the general HR practices. Ask about practices that might interfere with changing the process.	• What HR practices affect this process? Are there HR rules that will make it difficult to do certain things?
	• What HR practices need to change, and can they be changed, if we redesign this process? What are the organized-labor implications of any changes?
6. Identify the current human resource information systems (HRIS).	• What HRIS currently exist? What are the tracking systems and databases they use, and how do we access the data? Who normally has access to these data?

Example

The team discovers that a particular work group is understaffed. HR policy, however, will not allow a group to tap the resources of another department without first posting jobs. Furthermore, HR may determine who has access to certain information or how it is accessed. Sometimes this adds additional steps to the core process in question, and therefore increases its costs. In the newly designed process, the people who have access to certain information will be very different.

The team concludes that HR must be involved in the redesign effort. Since the newly designed process will restructure jobs, HR must support this change. The team decides that they need to confirm how work rules prevent access to information and whether or not this adds cost to the process being redesigned.

Sketch the Core Process

Purpose of this procedure

The purpose of this procedure is to help you model, or map, the core process. Process mapping is the basic building block of process redesign, and flowcharting is one of the basic tools. In recent years, however, there has been an explosion in computer software—specifically project management and activity-based software—that offers other tools you can use to model an organization's core process. As stated in the Guidelines, this book will focus on flowcharts. However, activity-based software tools can be highly effective in modeling a process. If you need specific guidance on how to create a flowchart, look at the book by Rummler and Brache (1991) or the one by Morris and Brandon (1993).

There are several ways to create and verify a flowchart. Keep in mind that flowcharting is an iterative process. The redesign team first creates a rough map, which will then be verified through interviews and observations and modified as necessary. This is the basic mapping procedure; in practice it's not always quite so linear. The team may not know all the steps in a process, and it may have to interview and observe while still creating the map.

When to use this procedure

Use this procedure whenever you design a new process. It is a crucial step that will help you to

- Understand how work currently gets done.

- Ensure that everyone involved in the redesign project operates within a common framework. It is important for the redesign team, as well as for the organization as a whole, to share a common view of the core process and to understand as much about the process as possible.

- Gain insight on how specific activities affect worker performance and organizational performance.

Terms you may not know

Physical environment   A place, of any size, where work occurs. Consists of the internal environment (i.e., offices, factories) and the external environment (i.e., states, countries).

Process map   A model of a business process. Can be a flowchart or a graphical representation from an activity-based or program management software package.

Guidelines

You want to keep the focus of the design effort on understanding the entire process, rather than on how beautifully you can model the process. Have the team sketch out all the steps in the process. (I like to use big index cards or self-stick notes and put one step on each one.) Initially some people may dislike the notion of sketching. Once they get started, however, they will find that it's fun. Remind them that architects use sketching as a primary tool to generate creative thought. And only after the sketches are done can the details be addressed.

Gerald Weinberg (1982, pp. 157, 159) describes the advantages of sketching as follows:

1. A sketch can be drawn much more quickly than a polished map. Since a sketch takes less time, people don't hesitate to throw it away and then try something else.

2. A sketch's "very roughness conveys important information about where [the redesign team is] in the design process."

3. Because a sketch doesn't give anyone an "unjustified feeling of precision," it won't "intimidate anyone who has an idea about changing something."

Use whatever materials and forms make sense to the group you are working with. Some teams use transparent acetate sheets to draw the process, allowing them to overlay more and more detail on the map as they gather additional information on the process's activities. Other teams use large self-stick notes to represent major activities. These can be moved around and changed quite easily. Other teams use a computer right from the start and make periodic printouts.

What to do

In creating a process map you are trying to capture how inputs are transformed into outputs. For a particular core process, you might trace information or a product as it moves through the system from start to finish.

Steps	Suggested Questions & Approaches
1. Define the major output of the entire process.	Have the team define the major output.
2. Identify the major activities that make up the process.	Ask the team to define from one to twenty major activities that must be performed to create this output.
3. Chart the flow of activities.	Have the team sketch how these activities relate to each other.

Example

A redesign team created the following flowchart. (This is an oversimplified chart, used here only to illustrate flowcharting. In redesigning a core process, a flowchart can easily cover an entire wall. We will continue to build on this basic chart in later examples.)

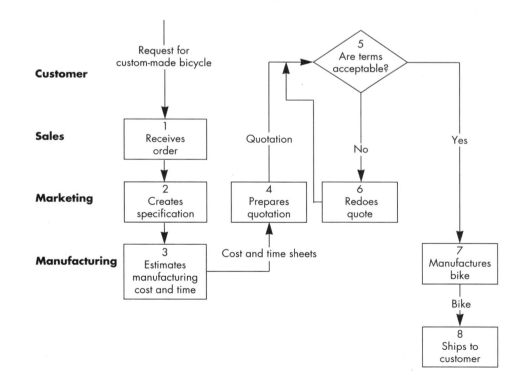

Sketch or List the Tasks That Make up Each Activity in the Process

Purpose of this procedure

You now have a sketch or macro picture of the process and a better understanding of the organization's customers' needs. Now it is time to get into the details by listing and mapping the tasks necessary for each particular activity. This will help you fully understand the current core process.

When to use this procedure

Use this procedure

- After you have sketched a preliminary flowchart.

- To modify the flowchart to incorporate the detailed information you collect.

- To gain insight on how specific activities and tasks affect worker and organizational performance.

Terms you may not know

Task A step or decision that is part of an activity necessary in creating an output.

Guidelines

Some suggest that you start with a list of all the tasks involved in creating an output and then group the tasks into activities. But in redesigning a core business process you may have hundreds, if not thousands of tasks to map, and the team can easily become overwhelmed by such detail. To avoid becoming paralyzed in the analysis stage, take the sketch flowchart or macro map you created earlier and break each of the boxes down as far as possible. Every time you break a box down, ask the team if there is enough detail on the map to fully understand what is happening. Strike a balance in the amount of detail you describe—do not include so much detail that it takes years to analyze it or it is immediately overwhelming.

As you are listing the tasks, make sure your team understands where in the process decisions are made, who makes these decisions, and why.

What to do

1. Pick one activity.

2. Define the major output of the activity.

   Ask the team.

3. Identify the major tasks that make up the activity.

   Have the team list and sequence the tasks. Stop when there is enough detail for the team to understand how the activity gets done. Make sure you include where decisions are made.

4. Chart the tasks.

   You may want to use a software program (e.g., activity-based software).

5. Repeat steps 1–4 for the remaining activities.

Example

The team identifies the output and tasks that make up activity no. 4, "Prepares Quotation." The major output is a custom-made bike shipped to the customer. A prerequisite output is a completed quotation. The tasks necessary to complete a quotation are illustrated below:

Chart the Flow of Information

Purpose of this procedure

Understanding what information is used and when, where, why, and how the user obtains and transmits that information to the next user are critical elements in understanding how information helps or hinders the accomplishment of tasks. This procedure will help you identify what information the system relies on in performing the process, where that information comes from, and in what form it exists. The procedure will give you a better understanding of how information flows through the current system.

When to use this procedure

Use this procedure after you have sketched or listed the tasks that make up the process.

Terms you may not know

Task A step or decision that is part of an activity necessary in creating an output.

What to do

Steps	Suggested Questions & Approaches
1. Interview and observe people performing an activity to determine what information is collected over the course of the process.	• What information is necessary for someone to perform this particular activity or step? • Why is this information necessary?
2. Determine how the information is transmitted.	• Where does this information originate? Where do you get it? Where do you send it?
3. Determine what task(s) the information is used in, how it is used, and where it is used.	• What would happen if this information were no longer available? • What are the key documents used in this process? • What documents are used to perform this particular step?
4. Chart where the information is used, by whom it is used, and how it gets transmitted.	• Who uses the information? See the example.

Example

The team records the information used in each activity in the process.

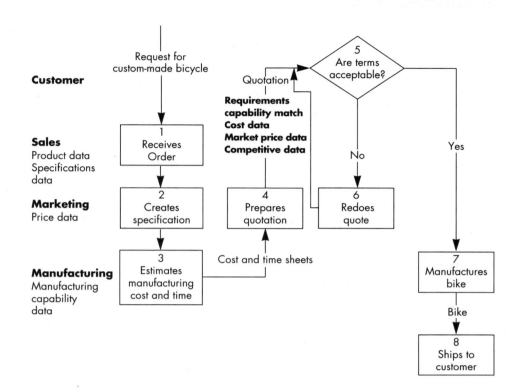

Next, the team charts how documents are used.

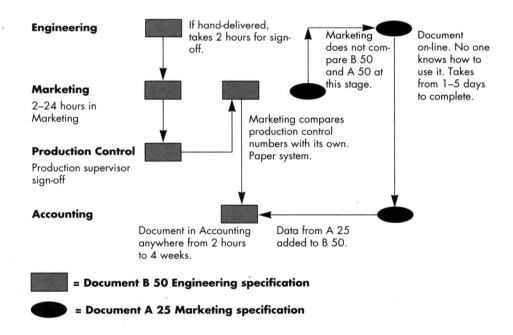

The team is beginning to capture the amount of time that passes while documents are waiting to be received.

Chart the Use of Technology

Purpose of this procedure

The purpose of this procedure is to determine what technology is currently used for the different activities and tasks in the process. Technology in general, and information technology in particular, is often a major element in process redesign. Technology can greatly improve an existing process or enhance the design of a new process. Designers should tie their plans for using technology to the information needs of the organization. It is important, however, not to confuse technology with information. Information is the critical ingredient in a successful business process; technology provides the tools to ensure that it is efficiently managed. This procedure will help you determine how technology is used to capture, store, and transmit the information necessary in performing the process.

When to use this procedure

Use this procedure after charting the information used in a process.

Terms you may not know

Technology Any hardware, software, or mechanized procedure that facilitates the transmittal of information and thereby affects work. Examples include a computer database, a filing system, a piece of equipment, a job aid.

What to do

Steps	Suggested Questions & Approaches
1. Interview people or walk through the process.	Use your process flowchart or your information chart to cue your questions and to give the team assignments about what to check into.
Ask what technology is used at different points in the process.	
2. Note the technology used to convert inputs into outputs.	
3. Note the technology used to transfer information.	
4. Note the technology used to support or achieve interfaces and relationships.	For example, what technology is used to transfer purchase order information into the financial accounting system.
5. Record what technology is used where.	Flag the various technologies on your current flowchart, or create a new chart. Use different-colored dots or pens.

Example

The redesign team notes the different technologies used over the course of the process and records them on their flowchart. They notice how much the process depends on paper and how often information must be re-created in order to be manipulated.

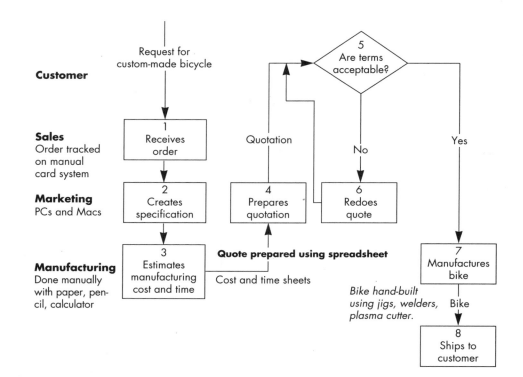

Identify Where Activities Occur

Purpose of this procedure

All processes are affected by the physical distribution of activities. For example, new products that are developed and manufactured at a single location are different from those developed in one country and manufactured in another. Work flows across time and space; this step will help your team understand how the physical space or environment affects the process you are modeling. You want to discover what (if any) processing time or costs are added when materials and information must be transported.

When to use this procedure

Use this procedure after you have identified all activities and tasks.

Terms you may not know

Environment   Where activities occur (location).

What to do

Steps	Suggested Questions & Approaches
1. Ask which activities are done in the same area (close together) and why.	
2. Ask which activities are done in different areas, countries, cities, buildings, floors, and such.	
3. Ask why certain activities are done in certain locations.	
4. Record where activities occur.	
5. List issues that arise because of the location of certain activities.	• How does location affect the performance of this activity? • Could this activity be performed somewhere else? Why or why not? • What would happen if this activity were located somewhere else?

Example

Using large self-stick notes, the team records on the original flowchart the locations where the work is performed.

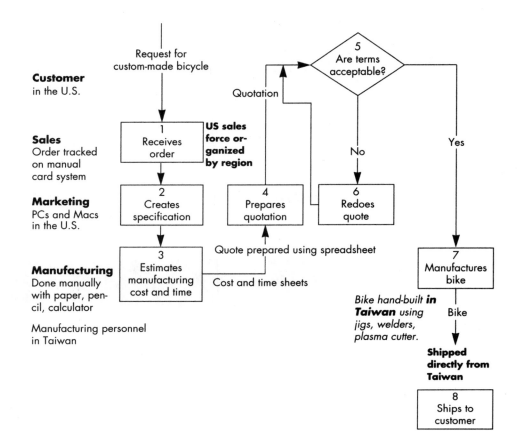

Add Performance Data

Purpose of this procedure

The purpose of this procedure is to understand how much a process costs in time, money, and resources. The team needs to understand the efficiency of the process—how long certain activities take, how much they cost, where the bottlenecks are, and so on.

When to use this procedure

Use this procedure

- After you have created a basic flowchart.
- Every time you map a process. Without this data you will not know how well the process currently performs.

Terms you may not know

Activity-based costing (ABC)   A process by which an organization determines how much certain activities cost the organization in dollar terms.

Cycle time   The time it takes the system to complete an activity or task (e.g., it takes five days on average, two days minimum, and eight days maximum to get an invoice signed).

Process time   The intrinsic time it takes to complete an activity or task (e.g., signing an invoice takes less than thirty seconds; it takes at most two hours to complete a quotation form).

Guidelines

You want to add time data, cost data, and any other type of data to your basic flowchart to help you understand the process. Time data is easier to add than cost and resource data. There are two critical time variables to capture: process time and cycle time.

There are two ways to calculate how long a particular process takes: 1) take *each activity* or task and add up the amount of time it takes to complete each one; 2) take *series of activities* or a series of tasks and add up the amount of time they take to complete.

You will most likely need to interview the people who perform the activities in order to understand how long they take to complete. People will either tell you specific times (two hours) or ranges (from two to six days).

If a range is given, immediately ask what some of the factors are that cause the activity to take a longer or shorter period of time.

Every output—usually a tangible entity (a report, a widget)—costs the organization something. Each output requires that a certain number of activities be performed. These activities require resources, and resources involve costs.

The objective is to understand the cost of the resources needed to complete each activity. Many organizations do not have readily available time or cost data for activities. Some organizations do not even know how to compile this type of data. It is important that you understand these variables. You may want to collect this data with the help of an expert. But if you have to, "guesstimate" costs.

Determine the performance measures for each output. There are four general performance measures:

1. Quantity of output. Quantity of output divided by resources used gives you a measure of efficiency. For example, producing ten widgets with eight dollars is not as efficient as producing ten widgets with two dollars.

2. Elapsed time. Elapsed time is an indirect measure of cost, quality, and customer satisfaction. The longer it takes to produce a product, the greater the resources it uses up (cost) and the greater the likelihood that it will need to be reworked (quality). In addition, longer process times or cycle times make it less likely that the organization will be able to respond to customer demands (customer satisfaction).

3. Quality. The more scrap or rework, the higher the cost.

4. Resource costs. While it's not necessary to quantify everyone's salary, you should get a sense of the value of the resources assigned to a particular activity. You might try to extrapolate people's salary from the posted salary range for their position. Make your best guess at where specific individuals fall within those ranges.

Before you start

1. Find out if the organization has any activity-based accounting data. If so, ask if you can use it.

2. Find out if the organization has done any time studies or has set performance standards for specific activities in terms of time or resource use. If so, ask if you can use them.

What to do

Steps	Suggested Questions & Approaches
1. Record process and cycle times for each task.	Ask the performers; they often know. If they don't know, they may be willing to collect the data for you. Provide them with a short worksheet so they can track their time. This data can also be entered in various types of software, which will allow you to make easier and faster calculations. You might also want to create a worksheet for yourself (see the example).
2. Identify the resources used for each activity or task.	See the book *Common Cents* (Turney, 1992). Get help from the finance person on the redesign team.
3. Assign (estimate) a cost for each of those resources.	
4. Assign performance measures, where possible, for each activity or task.	Try to reflect each of the four performance measures (quantity of output, elapsed time, quality, resource costs) for each of the activities on your process map, as best you can.

Example

A company has five quality inspectors. The two key resource costs associated with these inspectors are approximately $150,000 in salaries and benefits and $25,000 in overhead. If all five inspectors spend 75 percent of their time inspecting parts and 50 percent of the overhead is used, the cost of inspecting parts is $125,000 (.75 × $150,000 + .50 × $25,000).

The company produces 100 widgets per month. The costs associated with inspection are $10,400 per month ($125,000 ÷ 12). Therefore, inspection costs $104 per widget ($10,400 ÷ 100).

The redesign team develops the following worksheet and asks performers to fill it out over the course of a week.

Activity	Process Time	Cycle Time	Resources Needed (People, $, Etc.)	Comments

The team records this data on the flowchart shown here. They discover it takes over ten days from the time an order comes in until approval is given to start manufacturing, although the actual process time is only 6.5 hours.

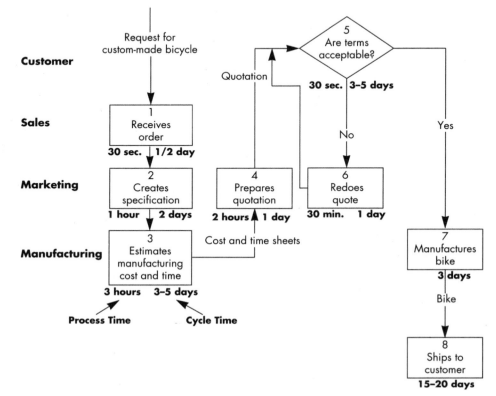

| Procedure 3.10 | **Determine Current Process Success Factors** |

Purpose of this procedure

Whenever you begin to change a process, you want to first understand what works well in the current process. You don't want to inadvertently leave out or remove a critical factor that makes a process successful. This procedure is used primarily in incremental redesign. However, teams involved in fundamental redesign can use parts of this procedure to get a good understanding of the current process.

When to use this procedure

Use this procedure after identifying process times, costs, and resources used.

What to do

Steps	Suggested Questions & Approaches
1. Determine how success is defined in the organization.	• You may want to interview people throughout the organization to get a wider perspective.
2. Identify factors that contribute to the success of the current process (activities, tasks, policies, etc.).	• Is the process successful?
	• How do we know when the process is successful? Why?
3. Identify factors that impede success in the current process.	• What makes the current process successful?
4. Identify the source or origin of both the positive and the negative factors in the current process.	• What does not work well in the current process?
	• Where do these positive and negative factors come from? Why are they a part of the current process?
5. Record the answers on a worksheet.	

Example

A redesign team conducts the following interview:

Q. How do you know when this process is successful?

A. If the customer receives the XJ7 on the required date with no quality issues.

Q. Given this definition, is this process successful as it currently exists?

A. Yes and no. We usually have three to five day's slippage, and our quality is at about one defect per thousand. So, technically speaking, this process is not successful.

The team charts the responses on the table like this:

What factors are contributing to the success of the current process?	Why?	What causes these factors?
The new database software is speeding up order entry and delivery.	It's an easy-to-learn package, and both sales representatives and shipping personnel can enter data quickly.	One of the reasons we got the system was because we were making many order entry mistakes.
What factors impede the success of the current process?	**Why?**	**What causes these factors?**
Our engineers always design from scratch. They never use ideas from other places. They don't even use the design rule database.	There's a "not invented here" mentality. The engineers want to design something new.	There's a heavy emphasis by the corporation on new product development, and no one has ever explained that improving on someone else's design is just as valuable as creating a completely new design. The reward system reinforces new products.

The team concludes that the new database program rewards people by allowing them to enter orders accurately and quickly—no more filling out stacks of forms. It also confirms that the corporation tends to reward only new ideas. Therefore, engineers do not focus on using current designs and improving them.

| Procedure 3.11 | **Verify the Process Map** |

Purpose of this procedure

This procedure will help you to identify any missing information. It will enable you to confirm your understanding of the process independently, by questioning others who are knowledgeable about the process and its outputs.

When to use this procedure

Use this procedure after you have mapped the process and identified its success factors.

Guidelines

There are two methodologies that are powerful tools for verifying your process map.

Method A

Have a manager who has been with the company for a long time—someone who has an understanding of the entire process—walk you or your team through the core cross-functional process from start to finish. (See Shapiro, Rangan, and Sviokla, 1992.) As you walk through the process, ask some of the questions listed in Method B.

In all companies there is an entity (usually an order) that travels through the system. Along the way it is modified by the people in the organization. For example, an order is generated, costs are estimated, the order is received and entered, the order is prioritized, the order is fulfilled, and there is after-sales service on the order. These processes often take months to complete..Spend several days or a couple of weeks walking through the steps to look at how an order gets transformed into a product. You will see the process that evolves from the order (conception of idea, design of idea, analyses of design, design into prototype, prototype into manufacturable pieces, and so on).

By observing behaviors and how work gets done, you will get from your "walk" a sense of the overall system and how the individual functions operate together to produce the output. This will give you a systems perspective of the process.

Method B

If you have a basic flowchart prepared, travel throughout the organization and interview as many people as possible who are affected by the core process you are redesigning. Ask them for their input. Given the size of the map, you may want to have people come to where you have the map posted and interview them there. Use the following questions:

- Is this map comprehensive?

- What are other key outputs not captured on this map?

- What activities lead to this output?

- What are the major inputs into these activities? (Think of inputs as both physical entities and information.)

- How is information tracked? On written specs? Paper invoices? What percentage of this information is automated?

- What technology is used to convert a particular input into an output? What equipment or job aids are used? Is a computer used?

- What are the major decisions made within the process? Where and when within the process are these decisions made? Who makes the decisions? How many people are part of the decision-making process? Who are they? Are their signatures required? When?

- How long does this step take? Why does it take this long? Is there a range? Why is there a range? Why does it sometimes take longer to perform a step?

- What is the cost of performing these activities? Can you give me an estimate?

- What are the problems you encounter in performing this step? What causes these problems?

- What are the roadblocks in this process?

- What are the strengths of this process? Why are we better at x (developing new products, getting orders to customers, etc.) than our competitors? What works? When we redesign, we want to make sure we build on our strengths.

- How do we know when this process is successful?

- Is this process successful as it currently exists? How do you know?

- If we said that we had to be five or twenty times faster in performing this process, with the same level of quality or better, what are the critical items we should eliminate or retain?

What to do

Steps	Suggested Questions & Approaches
1. Choose a method to verify your process map.	Your team may decide to use both methods.
2. Incorporate the data you gained as you verified your process map onto the map or in other documentation.	Your goal should be to create a comprehensive map and to develop a team that fully understands how the process functions.

Example

Order-to-invoice core cross-functional process. This flowchart models how one company takes an order, produces and ships its product, and invoices its customers. There are many more data regarding time, resources, and metrics that have not been added here. But this is a good example of a basic model of a core cross-functional process. See the next two pages.

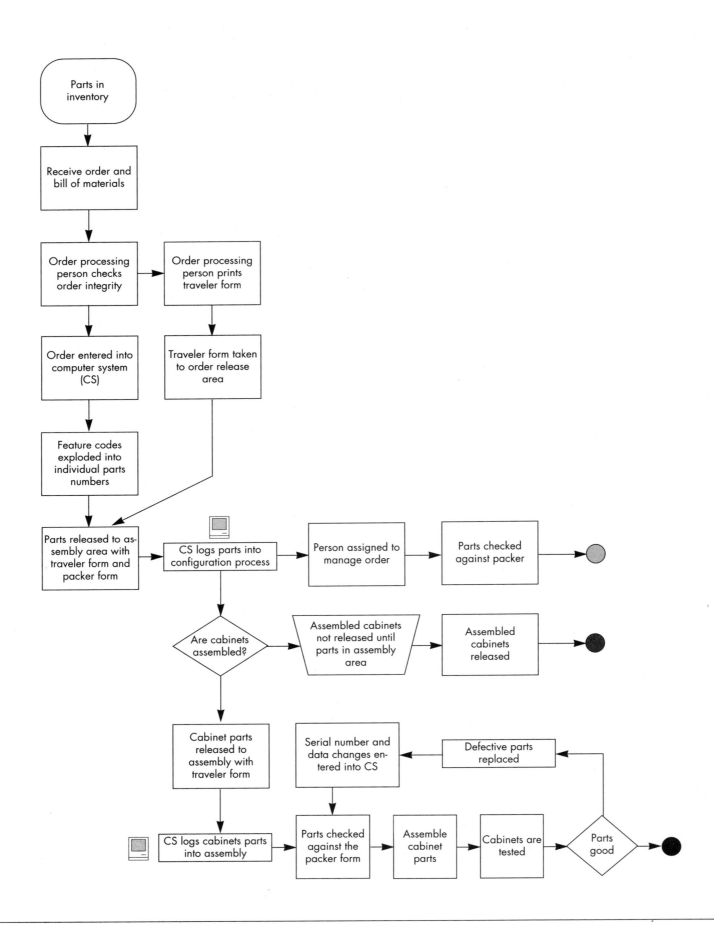

Parts in inventory

Receive order and bill of materials

Order processing person checks order integrity

Order processing person prints traveler form

Order entered into computer system (CS)

Traveler form taken to order release area

Feature codes exploded into individual parts numbers

Parts released to as-sembly area with traveler form and packer form

CS logs parts into configuration process

Person assigned to manage order

Parts checked against packer

Are cabinets assembled?

Assembled cabinets not released until parts in assembly area

Assembled cabinets released

Cabinet parts released to assembly with traveler form

Serial number and data changes en-tered into CS

Defective parts replaced

CS logs cabinets parts into assembly

Parts checked against the packer form

Assemble cabinet parts

Cabinets are tested

Parts good

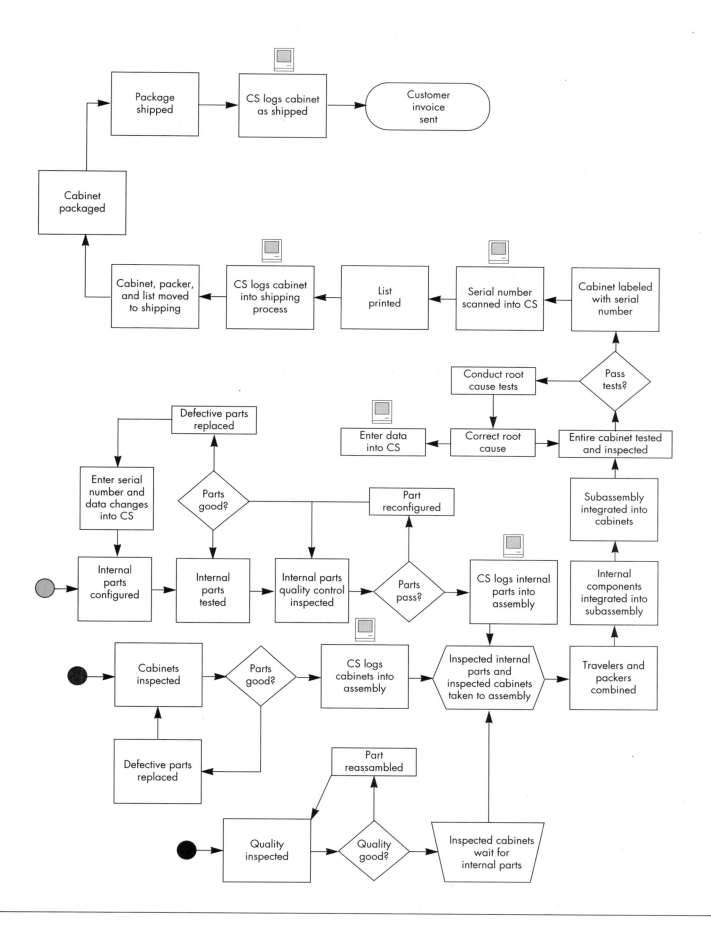

Prepare an Executive Summary Report

Purpose of this procedure

The purpose of this procedure is to capture and communicate what the redesign team has learned about the current system. The position paper (discussed in Chapter 2) focuses on why the redesign project is important. The executive summary report is a similar paper, but it focuses on what the team has learned. Sometimes this analysis turns into a presentation or other communication vehicle. The purpose of the paper is to demonstrate that you can communicate all the information you've collected to someone who is not on your team.

When to use this procedure

Use this procedure

- After you have completed and verified your process map.
- When you need to share your information-gathering efforts with a wide audience. This procedure is particularly useful in fundamental redesign projects.
- When you know that the organization has problems communicating.

Terms you may not know

Executive summary report   A review of what the team has learned, focused specifically on how the current process performs (cost and time metrics) and how this affects customers.

Guidelines

It is critical that you let top management know about your efforts in an efficient format. Provide enough detail so that they understand the process. Too much detail, however, will overwhelm them and will prompt them to begin engineering the specifics themselves. Furthermore, you will also want to communicate your findings to the rest of the organization, and for this a summary report is optimal.

Keep the report focused, concise, and comprehensive. Once the group has decided on the format, have one individual write a draft that will come back to the group for editing and modification. The presentation or paper should be written in such a way that you can present it to executive staff. Mention the essentials, but get ready for some specific questions. Your analysis will be questioned for accuracy, thoroughness, and specificity. You and your team will be challenged on whether you really understand the process. You will also need to present parts of the paper to the entire organization. Limit the paper or presentation to ten pages.

What to do

Steps	Suggested Questions & Approaches
1. Develop a format.	Make the format easy to read, concise, and geared toward an executive audience.
2. Assign one person to write the summary.	Having one person write the summary will accelerate its completion. The team will have the opportunity to critique and modify the summary before it is presented to the organization.
3. Check for accuracy.	
4. Practice making your presentation. Have them challenge the summary's data, methodology, and conclusions.	Have team members role-play the executive audience.
5. Combine your final summary with your position paper.	I. The Position Paper—Why We Need to Redesign II. The Summary—What We've Learned: The Performance of the Current Process
6. Integrate the executive summary into your overall communication plan.	

Example

Here is a possible table of contents for the current system summary paper or presentation:

I. Methodology Used to Understand the Current System

II. Summary of the Culture Survey (if done)

III. Support Systems (e.g., Finance, HR)

IV. The Core Process—Its Efficiency and Effectiveness

    a) What the Customer Values from this Process

    b) Time Metrics

    c) Cost Metrics

    d) Resource Metrics

    e) Current Technology Summary

V. Next Steps—Create the New Design; Timeline

CHAPTER 4

Creating the Simplest Possible Design to Solve the Business Problem

Purpose of this chapter

By this point your team should have developed a position paper that explains the need for the redesign, a map of the current cross-functional process, and a summary of your data-gathering efforts. You know the time and cost of each step as well as the time and cost of the entire process. You may also know who is responsible for each step.

At this stage you will either work with the current process map to improve or eliminate certain steps in the process (incremental redesign) or design a completely new process from scratch (fundamental redesign).

The procedures in this chapter will help you to achieve a "breakthrough" in performance. They will help you

1. Look at the accomplishments or major outputs indicated by your process map.

2. Determine if the accomplishments or outputs are necessary. If they *are* necessary, you should then

   - Look at all the activities that go into achieving them.

   - Challenge whether the activities are necessary.

   - Modify the activities to make the process more efficient.

   - Eliminate whole bodies of activities (steps).

   - Determine if there is another more efficient way to achieve the same accomplishments or outputs.

3. If accomplishments or outputs are *not* necessary, you should consider eliminating them and all the activities necessary for achieving them.

4. Link proposed changes to the financial and human resource systems.

5. Constantly communicate your progress and your efforts.

Your goal is to create a process that will close the overall performance gap. This is probably the most creative period in the redesign project. The creativity of the redesign team is now critical. The team needs to think "outside the box." The redesign team must constantly question if there is another, better way—if something unconventional will close the gap. Challenge current assumptions. Ask "what if?"

How is this chapter organized?

To determine:	Follow this procedure:
What the customer needs	Procedure 4.1—Confirm the Needs of the Customer
How big a change is needed	Procedure 4.2—Choose Incremental or Fundamental Redesign
What outcomes are required	Procedure 4.3—Identify the Accomplishments and Categorize the Activities
What the breakdowns in performance are	Procedure 4.4—Identify all Performance Gaps
The causes of the breakdowns	Procedure 4.5—Determine the Root Cause
What the choices are	Procedure 4.6—Generate Alternatives
The most appropriate choice	Procedure 4.7—Determine the Best Alternative
What an improved process will look like	Procedure 4.8—Sketch the Improved Process
What will be considered a success in a new design	Procedure 4.9—Confirm the Objectives and Effectiveness Factors of the New Design
How to create radical alternatives	Procedure 4.10—Engage in Breakthrough Thinking
How to begin the new design	Procedure 4.11—Create a General Sketch of the New Process
How what's rewarded and tracked must change	Procedure 4.12—Determine How the Current Financial System Needs to Change to Support the New Design
How HR must change	Procedure 4.13—Determine How the Current Human Resource System Needs to Change to Support the New Design
If the new process will work	Procedure 4.14—Evaluate the New Design
How the new process will affect the organization	Procedure 4.15—Design the Organization Chart
What to present to others	Procedure 4.16—Prepare for Executive and Steering Committee Presentations

Recommended approach

The recommended approach is as follows:

1. Start with Procedures 4.1 and 4.2.
2. For incremental redesign use Procedures 4.3–4.8.
3. For fundamental redesign use Procedures 4.9–4.15.
4. End with Procedure 4.16.

Guidelines

Incremental and fundamental redesign have been presented in this book as two separate options, but it is perhaps better to think of them as two ends of a continuum. I have seen groups take a "blank sheet of paper approach" to redesigning a process but not end up redesigning the entire organization. Would this be called reengineering the business? Probably not. However, it was closer to the fundamental end of the continuum than to the incremental end.

Incremental Redesign   Fundamental Redesign

Let me give you an example of a change effort I consider to be closer to the fundamental end of the continuum, but not as fundamental as process or business reengineering. I was recently working with a group on improving the cycle time of a process. The goal was to reduce the cycle time tenfold, from ninety days to nine days. We started looking at the current process: how long it takes, what we would need to do, and so on. The effort began to bog down early on. People started discussing the details of improving a particular machine or a certain process. Some team members became frustrated—they knew we would never achieve a tenfold improvement using our customary ways of thinking. So we decided to change the focus of the meetings. I gave the team these instructions: "As you know, we're looking at a major reduction in cycle time. We're never going to get there unless we become radical about our thinking. Let's start with a blank white sheet of paper. If we had to design this process from scratch, what would you do?"

"Outside the box" thinking

People really liked the idea. Their first question was, "Why do we need to be constrained by nine days? Why don't we say it will take zero days?" Now, even though this sounds quite radical, people honestly believed it could be done—not without a lot of effort and hard work, but it could be done. The group of fifteen people divided into two groups and spent the next few sessions brainstorming. After the brainstorming, a team was chosen to take all the ideas and work with another team to come up with specific recommendations and a roadmap for how to bring the cycle time down to zero days. This procedure represented "outside the box" thinking at its best. We would have never stumbled upon the ideas we came up with if we had kept looking at the current process. This was not a fundamental redesign effort, but it shows that if you give people a blank piece of paper they do begin to think "outside the box." They shove limitations aside.

Without a mandate to think radically and redesign from scratch, people will keep thinking within the current paradigm. They will wonder if they can question the existence of a policy or be skeptical that anything will really happen. Their true creative force is never fully released, and consequently the change they design does not fundamentally improve the position of the company. But if you give a group of individuals a goal, allow them complete freedom in designing a process to achieve the goal, and free them from habitual ways of thinking and entrenched bureaucratic structures—in short, if you tell them nothing is sacred—they can achieve phenomenal results. By tapping into the creative powers of a cross-functional redesign team composed of the organization's best people, you will be able to create a design that clearly addresses a far-reaching critical business issue.

Going back to how you think

Peter Senge (1992, p. 53) writes that "for most players of the game, the deepest insight usually comes when they realize that their problems, and their hopes for improvement, are inextricably tied to how they think." This is a pivotal concept. In redesign one of the key tasks is to determine a new process. But this must begin back at an earlier point. Whether your charter is for incremental or fundamental change, you will begin by building on your current process and your current ways of thinking.

But it's not always easy to move beyond this stage, because people are naturally wary of change. Fundamental change in particular is inherently risky—jobs change, education changes, strategies change, the entire culture changes. People are even more likely to feel constrained or to retreat into familiar ways of thinking. You want to be sure your redesign team is free to develop the best possible solutions; it is vital that their most creative ideas be allowed to surface. Therefore, while they should learn from the current process, they must not be constrained by the current way of doing things. Radical thinking is in order—anything goes. The objective is to get people to think outside of their current "box." Their creativity must be given a clean slate to work with.

Results

If you follow the recommendations and procedures in this chapter, you should achieve the following results:

- An appreciation for the potential gain that moving to a new design can offer.

- A model of how the new process should function.

- An understanding of the ramifications of the new design on financial and human resource systems.

- An executive presentation that will inform top management of all the work completed by the redesign team up to the point of implementation.

For More Information

Davenport, T. H. *Process Innovation—Reengineering Work through Information Technology.* Boston, Mass.: Harvard Business School Press, 1993.

De Bono, E. *Serious Creativity.* New York: Harper Business, 1992.

Goal/QPC. *The Memory Jogger: A Pocket Guide of Tools for Continuous Improvement.* Goal/QPC, Methuen, Mass., 1988.

Morris, D., and Brandon, J. *Reengineering Your Business.* New York: McGraw-Hill, 1993.

Rummler, G. A., and Brache, A. P. *Improving Performance.* San Francisco: Jossey-Bass, 1991.

Shapiro, B. P., Rangan, V. K., and Sviokla, J. J. "Staple Yourself to an Order." *Harvard Business Review* (July–August 1992), 113–122.

Smith, P. G., and Reinertsen, D. G. *Developing Products in Half the Time.* New York: Van Nostrand Reinhold, 1991.

VanGundy, A. B. Jr., *Techniques of Structured Problem Solving.* New York: Van Nostrand Reinhold, 1988.

Confirm the Needs of the Customer

Purpose of this procedure

The purpose of this procedure is to help you better understand how the process you are redesigning affects the organization's customers. Understanding what customers want is the starting point of redesign. The key is to find out what matters to your customers and how much the process you are redesigning contributes to what is important to them. Too often a process is redesigned and the customers do not notice any change. Your team should be clear on how redesigning the process will affect performance and whether customers will recognize improvement.

When to use this procedure

Use this procedure before you begin to modify the current process or design a new process from scratch.

Before you start

1. Identify who the customers are. Start with these questions:

   - Who are the organization's customers?

   - Who are the customers affected by this process (both internal and external customers)?

   - How many customers are there? How profitable is each customer? How much revenue is generated by each customer?

   - Which current customers are most important?

   - Who are the potential customers that will be critical to the organization's success in the next five years?

2. Develop a shared understanding of what your customers want. Work backwards from there to design a process that will meet those customer needs in the most efficient and effective manner. Ask questions like these:

   - Where does the organization fall in the supplier-to-customer chain?

   - Who are your customers' customers, and what do they want?

   - What are your customers' strengths and weaknesses?

   - Who are your customers' competitors? What threats do they pose?

   - How are your customers doing financially?

   - What is their market share?

   - What are your customers' problems and concerns?

3. Come back to this data to help you gauge how well your organization's core process satisfies your customers' wants and needs.

What to do

Steps	Suggested Questions & Approaches
1. Choose which customers to focus on.	Use a set of criteria to determine which customers you intend to focus on (the largest revenue generators, the up-and-coming customers, etc.)
2. Find out what your customers want.	Use the sample form on the next page as a guide. If necessary, go directly to your customer or to the customer's customer. Talk to them about their own operations as well as how they perceive your organization.
3. List the need that customers did not articulate.	The team might brainstorm a list or use some of the insights they gained while interviewing customers.
4. List the criteria the new design must meet to satisfy the customer.	

Example

The following conversation illustrates a customer interview. A customer says she wants a cup with a strong handle.

> **You:** Why a strong handle? I'm really trying to understand your needs, so I'm going to ask "why" a lot. I hope you don't mind.
>
> **Customer:** No, go right ahead. I think a cup with a strong handle would be a lot easier to grab hold of.
>
> **You:** Why should the cup be easy to grab hold of?
>
> **Customer:** I want to be able to grab it with one hand. And if it contains a hot liquid, a strong handle won't get too hot—that's important.
>
> **You:** Can you explain why these features are important?
>
> **Customer:** Well, I like to drink my coffee in the morning while I drive to work, and these features would make it easier.

A conversation such as this will give you a much better understanding of what the customer wants, including some preliminary indicators of the customer's ultimate use for the product. With this information you can now speculate what other features might make the product even more desirable to the customer (e.g., wide base so it doesn't tip over, narrow top so it doesn't spill, dishwasher safe).

Customer name _____

Primary or secondary customer? _____

	1	2	3	4	5	6
	Answer	Why is the answer in column #1 important?	Why is the answer in column #2 important?	Why is the answer in column #3 important?	Why is the answer in column #4 important?	Why is the answer in column #5 important?
What the customer says he or she wants						
What you think the customer expects that was not said						
What you think would excite the customer						

Choose Incremental or Fundamental Redesign

Purpose of this procedure

The purpose of this procedure is to help you determine the appropriate redesign methodology. Should you redesign incrementally or fundamentally? In many cases this will depend on what your sponsor believes and on the magnitude of the performance gap. Executives are often unwilling to charter a fundamental redesign effort from the start—the risk is perceived as too high. However, after the business process has been modeled and management understands the significance of the issue, they are often more willing to charter a fundamental redesign effort. In many cases the team will have to be rechartered, and there may be a new sponsor as well.

When to use this procedure

Use this procedure

- After you have modeled the current business process and have a good understanding of how it performs.
- While you are clarifying the request at the beginning of the project.

Terms you may not know

Incremental redesign   Improving elements of the current process. A smaller-scale change.

Fundamental redesign   Designing a completely new process from scratch. Sometimes called reengineering. Larger-scale change.

What to do

Steps	Suggested Questions & Approaches
1. Interview the sponsor and other top executives to determine whether incremental or fundamental redesign is more appropriate.	Address both process-specific issues and cultural issues in the interview. Process-specific: • Are there many problems in the execution of this cross-functional process? • Is the process currently fragmented? • If every step in the current process were improved, would there still be a problem? • Is there a lack of accountability for the entire process (is no single person accountable)? Do items get "thrown over the wall" to the next operation or function? Cultural: • Would you say that the level of improvement required represents a paradigm shift in the organization? In other words, will the organization need to operate under different assumptions? Will it need to change its culture? • Will other systems and departments (e.g., HR, Finance) need to change? • Are we on a "burning platform"? (Is the business in major trouble?)

Steps	Suggested Questions & Approaches
2. Compare their responses.	The more "yes" answers, the greater the probability that fundamental redesign is necessary.
3. Present findings to the sponsor.	
4. Agree on a plan of action.	If fundamental redesign is necessary, the sponsor may need to educate other executives regarding the impact of this project. Furthermore, he or she will have to involve the top executive.
5. Use the appropriate set of procedures.	For incremental redesign, see Procedures 4.3–4.8 and 4.16. For fundamental redesign, see Procedures 4.9–4.16.

| Procedure 4.3 | **Identify the Accomplishments and Categorize the Activities** |

Purpose of this procedure

The purpose of this procedure is to identify the accomplishments (outputs) of the process and the activities that lead to those accomplishments. In a cross-functional process there are many accomplishments that must be achieved.

When to use this procedure

Use this procedure

- When incremental redesign is desired.

- When you have a basic understanding of the current system.

- When you are ready to begin improving the current process (closing the performance gaps).

Terms you may not know

Waiting/Queued   A holding or retaining activity (e.g., holding cabinets while other parts are assembled).

Altering   An operationally transforming activity. The product or the information is altered (e.g., cabinet parts are assembled).

Inspecting   An activity that reviews or checks the output of a previous activity (e.g., inspecting assembled cabinets).

Transporting   An activity in which something (either a product or information) must be moved from one place to another before it can be altered (e.g., moving cabinets to a facility for assembly).

Accomplishment (Output)   The tangible, measurable, specific result of an activity.

Before you start

1. Assemble worksheets for listing and classifying activities. (See the example.)

2. Have your process map and performance data available.

3. Decide whether you intend to purchase an activity-based or program management software program, use a spreadsheet, or categorize the activities manually.

What to do

Steps	Suggested Questions & Approaches
1. List the accomplishments.	Use your process map.
2. List and categorize the activities.	Use the WAIT system of classifications:
	W = Waiting, on hold, in storage
	A = Being altered
	I = Being inspected or checked
	T = In transit
	(See the next page.)
3. List the associated process time, cycle time, cost, department, responsibility, and technology for each activity.	(See the next page.)
4. Create a summary sheet.	(See the next page.)

Accomplishment/Output	Activity	WAIT Category	Process Time	Cycle Time (min.)	Cycle Time (max.)	Cycle Time (avg.)	Cost ($ min.)	Cost ($ max.)	Cost ($ avg.)	Dept. or Function	Responsible	Technology	Comments
Quotation	1. Check accuracy	I	2 hrs.	5 hrs.	1 day	7 hrs.	400	460	500	Mktg.	John	Spread-sheet	Has to wait for 3 hrs. for mfg. cost data
	2. Wait until additional costs are estimated	W											
	3. Analyze competitor's prices	A											
	4. Determine markup	A											

Identify All Performance Gaps

Purpose of this procedure

The purpose of this procedure is to identify any activities—in terms of time and costs, and quality and volume of outputs—that contribute to not meeting the customer's needs.

When to use this procedure

Use this procedure

- When incremental redesign is desired.
- After you have gained a basic understanding of the current system.
- After you have categorized the process's activities.

Guidelines

There are several techniques you can use to determine where performance gaps exist. Brainstorming is one possibility, but observing how work is done and looking at actual performance data is often more revealing (see Goal/QPC, 1988).

Terms you may not know

Performance gap   The difference between current performance and desired performance.

At the end of this procedure you might have a long list of performance gaps that directly affect the process. Not all of these problems will have the same impact, however. If you target certain gaps to close first, you will have a greater impact on the critical business issue. Choose the gaps that have the largest impact on solving the problem first (see Procedure 4.5). This way the organization will see that something serious is happening, and it will be able to build on that success. You might eventually have to cose all the gaps in order to achieve the overall goal. But at this point it is important to identify the most serious gaps and to determine what to work on first.

What to do

Steps	Suggested Questions & Approaches
1. Create a gap analysis worksheet.	(See the example.)
2. Describe the desired performance for each accomplishment.	
3. Describe actual current performance.	
4. Note where a gap exists.	If possible, translate the gap into terms of time and money.
5. Group the gaps in terms of their impact on the critical business issue.	

Example

A redesign team might use a gap analysis worksheet like this:

Accomplishment	Verification of Specifications	Defect-Free Cabinets
Desired performance	All specifications verified by engineer before sending to manufacturing.	Have cabinet assemblers do inspections (no need for separate inspectors).
Actual performance	80% of specifications not verified by engineer	Two people spend 1 hour per cabinet at cost of $100.
Gap (if any)	80%	Hourly labor cost of $50, plus inspector overhead
Significance of gap	Lost time due to necessity to redo work; estimated cost of $3,000/week	Extra time, money
Is gap critical?	Yes	Yes
Root cause	Engineer does not know how to verify the specs.	Management's desire to have separate inspectors. Assemblers never held accountable for defects.
Best alternative	Work with manufacturing to develop a job aid that will allow engineer to verify specs.	Retrain inspectors Educate management Hold assemblers accountable
Can or will an activity be eliminated?	No	Yes
Job(s) affected	Engineer and manufacturing operator	Inspector and assembler
Activity category	Inspect (I)	Inspect (I)

| Procedure 4.5 | **Determine the Root Cause** |

Purpose of this procedure

The purpose of this procedure is to identify the performance gaps that, if eliminated, will have the greatest impact on the overall process.

When to use this procedure

Use this procedure after all performance gaps have been identified.

Terms you may not know

Cause-and-effect diagram   A diagram that explains the relationship between an effect and all of its possible causes.

Performance data   Data that the organization has or can collect regarding performance (e.g., Pareto charts, histograms, control charts, run charts, scatter diagrams).

Root cause   The essential, fundamental reason that something happens or does not happen.

Guidelines

There are several methods for determining the root cause:

- Observe the activity in action.

- Look at performance data about the specific accomplishment.

- Brainstorm possible causes.

Use these categories to structure your investigations or to spark ideas: Methods, Machinery, People, Materials. Alternatively, you could use a model developed by Rummler and Brache (1991). They have identified key causes for a process step not being performed (see table on the next page). Test Rummler and Brache's model against your situation. Chances are, one of the key causes they identify will be the root cause of your problem.

Rummler and Brache's key causes for nonperformance

Cause	Topic Area
1. The desired performance is not identified, appropriate, or communicated.	Accomplishment
2. The necessary input is not received, not on time, or not up to standard.	Input
3. There are insufficient materials, equipment, or staff.	Resources
4. Steps are redundant, missing, or inadequate.	Process
5. There are no consequences (positive or negative) for performance.	Consequences
6. No feedback is given regarding good or bad performance.	Feedback
7. The performer does not have the skill or knowledge necessary to perform as desired.	Knowledge
8. The performer is not capable of doing the job.	Capacity
9. The performer does not know when to perform or is expected to make responses that are in conflict.	Interference

What to do

Steps	Suggested Questions & Approaches
1. Decide how to identify the root cause.	See Guidelines.
2. Develop a cause-and-effect chart.	See Goal/QPC (1988).
3. Whenever possible, verify the cause with data.	Can the cause be verified with available data? How difficult is it to verify?
4. Rank according to criticality.	Determine how critical you think the cause is with regard to the problem you have identified. Rank the cause's criticality on a scale of 1 to 3 (1 not critical, 3 very critical).
5. Note the degree of difficulty involved to remove or fix the root cause.	

Example

The team working on the quotation process (for the custom-made bike) used a fish-bone diagram, otherwise known as a cause-and-effect diagram, to identify the root cause.

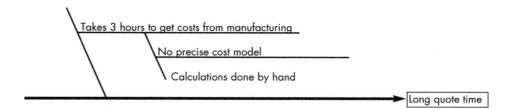

Takes 3 hours to get costs from manufacturing

No precise cost model

Calculations done by hand

Long quote time

Can be verified with available data; Not difficult to verify; Critical (3); Not difficult to fix.

Procedure 4.6	## Generate Alternatives

Purpose of this procedure

The purpose of this procedure is to determine the solution for closing a specific gap. The goal is to reduce or eliminate all W, I, and T (waiting, inspecting, transporting) activities and optimize the A (altering) activities.

It's important that you recognize that there are different levels of performance gaps. The critical business issue is the macro gap; it is usually made up of several micro gaps. You need to keep the entire system in mind as you develop alternatives for either type of gap.

When to use this procedure

Use this procedure after you have identified the micro performance gaps and their root causes.

Terms you may not know

Benchmark An assessment of how other organizations have dealt with a similar issue.

Guidelines

Define a benchmark to help measure your efforts against the experience of others. Look at what other companies have done to improve a similar core process. Do not constrain yourself by focusing only on your own industry. The objective is to find organizations that have successfully redesigned similar core processes, regardless of their area of specialization.

Benchmarks are a useful tool, but be wary of allowing your thinking to become limited by them. You might miss a revolutionary and effective solution if you are too focused on the experience of another company. Use benchmarks to help stimulate your thinking, but do not allow them to define your thinking.

If you are familiar with brainstorming techniques, use the technique you are most familiar with and supplement it with the following techniques as needed.

Techniques

Free association. Write down something directly related to the problem (e.g., speed). Write at least twenty thoughts that come to mind regarding the topic. At this point, don't worry about how relevant they are to solving the problem (e.g., light, computers, drugs, little, short, no paper, etc.). Select the thoughts that might be relevant to the problem and generate ideas. If nothing proves relevant, try a new topic.

If you are not familiar with brainstorming techniques, there are a variety of resources available that offer guidance. The best book I have found is by Arthur B. VanGundy, Jr. (1988). It's best if you can get the team off-site or in a secluded area where you won't be disturbed by phone calls and other interruptions. Also, creativity is enhanced by a relaxed, playful atmosphere. Most group problem-solving techniques use brainstorming as an initial stimulus to get ideas flowing. It's important to manage the brainstorming process in order to make it more effective.

"What If." Mention to the redesign team that to get the best ideas you suggest playing "What If." With your process map available for reference, ask these questions:

- What if we didn't do this?
- What if the technology used in the process radically changed?
- What if the information used in the process were instantly available to everyone involved?
- What if there were no more sign-offs?
- What if unlimited resources were available?
- What if no people were available to do this?
- What if this had to be done one hundred times faster?
- What if this activity were performed by _____ (by John, by Joe, by computer, manually, by Marketing, etc.)?
- What if we eliminated all of these steps? What would be the consequences to the entire process?
- What if this were *your* company—how would *you* do it?

What to do

Steps	Suggested Questions & Approaches
1. Choose a method of generating alternatives.	See the suggested methods under Guidelines.
2. Identify alternatives.	Ask how the process, the accomplishment, and the corrective measures would change if we used different technology, a different sequence of activities, or other resources.
3. Rank the alternatives.	Rank the proposed changes according to the difficulty that would be encountered in implementing them.
4. Select the alternatives that are most feasible.	

Example

A redesign team might come up with this series of alternatives to correct the problem of completing and routing work orders.

Alternative	Not Difficult to Implement	Somewhat Difficult	Difficult	Very Difficult
Rewrite the system	☑	☐	☐	☐
Purchase a new system	☐	☐	☑	☐
Eliminate work orders	☐	☐	☐	☑

Determine the Best Alternative

Purpose of this procedure

The purpose of this procedure is to identify those alternatives that will produce the greatest return, where the benefits will outweigh the costs and the one that meets most of the criteria.

When to use this procedure

Use this procedure after you have generated an initial list of alternatives.

Terms you may not know

Cost-to-benefit ratio   The quantitative and qualitative trade-off between what something will cost versus what it will bring.

Guidelines

If a more sophisticated financial cost-benefit analysis of a specific alternative is desired, use the expertise of the team member from Finance, seek help from the Finance department, or use an outside expert.

Before you start

- Assemble all the alternatives
- Familiarize yourself with the different tools available to help you choose the best alternative (see VanGundy, 1988).

What to do

Steps	Suggested Questions & Approaches
1. Complete a cost-versus-benefit chart.	See the example.
2. Brainstorm possible financial costs for each alternative.	Be sure to include implementation costs. In some cases, the group may not have all the cost information it needs. Assign a member to gather the data.
3. Brainstorm possible financial benefits for each alternative.	In some cases, the group may not have all the benefits information it needs. Assign a member to gather the data.
4. Develop the criteria you intend to use to rank the alternatives.	These might include cost, length of time to implement, and such. Some criteria may be "show stoppers" (i.e., if not met, the alternative cannot be used).
5. Evaluate and rank each alternative according to the criteria you deem most important.	See the example.
6. Choose the best alternative	Choose the alternative that provides greatest benefit at least cost.

A redesign team might use a chart like this to record and compare the potential cost and benefits of each alternative. In the majority of cases this type of analysis will suffice.

Alternative	Financial Benefits	Nonfinancial Benefits	Financial Costs	Nonfinancial Costs
1				
Total				
2				
Total				
3				
Total				

A chart such as this can be used to rank each alternative in terms of specific criteria. Each alternative is assessed on whether it meets a certain criterion.

Criteria/Constraints	Alternative 1		Alternative 2	
	Yes	No	Yes	No
< $10,000 (must meet)	✓			✓
Paper-less	✓			✓
Take < 1 hour	✓		✓	
Cost of Time < $500		✓	✓	
Total	3	1	2	2

Sketch the Improved Process

Purpose of this procedure

This procedure enables you to see what the process would look like if various improvements were added. It will help you identify any upstream or downstream consequences—since you are now rebuilding the process, you must be especially aware of how it flows within the system. The solutions you implement will have consequences elsewhere. Integrating solutions into a new process map will help you maintain a systems perspective and make sure that everything in the new design works in concert.

When to use this procedure

Use this procedure after you have selected the best alternatives.

Before you start

1. Review Procedures 3.4–3.9.
2. Plan to use the same types of tools as those discussed in Chapter 3.

What to do

Steps	Suggested Questions & Approaches
1. Sketch the new process.	Draw a new process map, based on the current map, that eliminates all the gaps you identified previously. Keep in mind all of the alternatives you identified as closing specific gaps. Use your gap analysis worksheet (4.4) if you created one.
2. Chart the flow of information.	The flow of information can be integrated into your new process map.
3. Chart the use of technology.	The use of technology can be integrated into your new process map.
4. Identify key accomplishments/outputs throughout the process.	For example, a completed quotation is a key accomplishment within the process.
5. Add performance criteria.	Use your gap analysis worksheet (4.4) if you created one. Understand how you will measure whether the accomplishment meets the performance criteria. How will you know that an accomplishment was achieved to the appropriate level of quality, time, cost, and such?
6. Prepare your report and summary for presentation.	Go to Procedure 4.16 at the end of this chapter. You may need to include your gap analysis worksheet (4.4) if you created one, and your cost/benefit analysis, since this is focused on incremental redesign.

Procedure 4.9	**Confirm the Objectives and Effectiveness Factors of the New Design**

Purpose of this procedure

The purpose of this procedure is to identify what factors (e.g., cost, speed, quality, volume) to emphasize when developing a new design.

When to use this procedure

Use this procedure

- After the decision has been made to fundamentally redesign the process.

- Before you begin to design a new process from scratch.

- After you have drawn a current "as is" process map.

- After you have identified the time, costs, and resources used in the process.

Guidelines

Processes that emphasize speed are different from those that emphasize cost, and both of these are different from processes that emphasize product performance. There are always trade-offs between quality, time, and cost. The redesign team needs to consider these variables. What factor are you going to emphasize?

Factor	Criteria
Product quality	Accuracy; completeness; reliability; ease of use, etc.
Development speed	Cycle time; process time; W, I, T, and A times
Process productivity	Quantity and rate; output over time
Process costs	Labor; materials; equipment; activities, etc.

The best way to understand the trade-offs you will face is to model the economic impact of the new process or the different variations of a process. For a new-product-development process, for example, the team may want to calculate the cost of delay (see Smith and Reinertsen, 1991).

Before you start   Assemble and use the data you gathered in Procedure 4.1 (customer requirements) and at the end of Procedure 3.10 (success factors).

What to do

Steps	Suggested Questions & Approaches
1. Decide what factors the new process needs to emphasize.	Emphasize cost, speed, productivity, quality, product performance, or accuracy.
2. Identify the desired basic attributes of the new process.	For example, should the new process eliminate "silos," switch from paper to electronic data transfer, require no more than two signatures per document, provide every engineer with a separate workstation, etc.
3. Establish a set of criteria for measuring each factor in the new process.	See Guidelines.
4. Determine the end accomplishment and most significant outputs of the new process.	The end accomplishment could be a prototype shipped to the customer. Significant outputs of the process could include a business case, specification, completed design, project approval, resource plan, and launch plan.
5. Determine standards for each criteria.	How many errors, how fast, at what cost, etc.

Example

A redesign team decides that development speed and process costs are the most important factors to address. A key attribute required is that there be no design changes after the first formal review (cycle time and labor costs are currently high due to design changes). The new process must reduce cycle time by at least 75 percent. Estimated savings are $150,000 per program. The end accomplishment is a point-of-sales kit. The more significant outputs are an initial design, a mock-up, and a prototype. The standards they decide on for these outputs are as follows:

Outputs	*Standards*
Initial Design	• Meet quality requirements
	• Create in < 25 days
Mock-up	• No more than two changes to design
Prototype	• No design changes
	• Create in < 3 weeks
	• Must be manufacturable

Procedure 4.10	## Engage in Breakthrough Thinking

Purpose of this procedure

To design a new process that will achieve a breakthrough in performance, you must first achieve a breakthrough in thinking. The design team needs to break out of its current way of thinking and develop a process that will be truly revolutionary.

When to use this procedure

Use this procedure after you have identified the objectives and effectiveness factors of the new design.

Terms you may not know

Visual imagery   A problem-solving technique that uses visual props

Process measures   Measures that focus on the performance of the process (cycle time, cost of all activities, etc.)

System-oriented   Looking at the interaction of all the pieces, not just one element.

Technology-enhanced   Using information technology or any other type of technology to achieve fundamental shifts in performance.

Before you start

Review Procedure 4.6.

Guidelines

There are a variety of techniques you can use to help you break out of habitual ways of thinking (see VanGundy, 1988, and De Bono, 1992).

"What if" scenarios and free association exercises. See Procedure 4.6.

Reversals. Identify and list all the statements under which the system or process currently operates. Then take each of these statements and reverse them. This will help you stimulate thought and break out of conventional thinking. For example, restaurants serve food to people. Reverse that statement to its opposite and say that restaurants don't serve food to people.

Fantasy or wishful thinking. Ask the team to pretend that they are in another place or time. For example, tell them it is the year 2050. They are part of an underwater colony and must redesign the process to work in that environment. Or tell them they are now part of a shoe company instead of an insurance company. Or have each member of the team state what he or she would like to see if he or she could have any wish.

Fresh look. This is the simple technique of inviting an outsider or outsiders to one of your brainstorming sessions. An outsider can be defined in any way. The intent is to get a fresh look at your issues. Invite someone from a different industry, from a small entrepreneurial firm, someone who has nothing to do with business. As you begin your brainstorming session, make sure your team captures and listens to the ideas of these "outsiders."

Visual imagery. This is a variation on traditional brainstorming techniques. It can be used in conjunction with many other techniques. Instead of having the team work with written or verbal communication, have them work with visual tools. Place a piece of large butcher paper on the wall and ask team members to draw their ideas as they describe them. No one has to be an artist—simple sketches will suffice. By combining written and verbal cues with pictures you can develop a more playful, creative environment.

What to do

Steps	Suggested Questions & Approaches
1. Select a technique.	See Guidelines.
2. Schedule several days or more.	Go ahead with the session even if you can't get the full team together. The objective is to get people off-site and to get them to stop thinking about day-to-day concerns.
3. Prepare the participants.	Explain to the team ahead of time what you are going to do. Explain that you will be using one or two activities to enhance creative thought. Have them come casually dressed.
4. Set ground rules ahead of time.	People should not use cellular phones or try to manage the office while they are in the meeting. Hopefully, the team will be full time and you won't have to worry about interruptions. Creative time does not mean unfocused or constantly interrupted time.
5. Hold the session.	You may want to use a trained facilitator in the selected technique. This frees everyone on the team to create. You may also want to invite some people who are "outsiders," who have not worked with your team to stimulate thinking.

Create a General Sketch of the New Process

Purpose of this procedure

The purpose of this procedure is to depict the new design so that it can be evaluated.

When to use this procedure

Use this procedure after the team has generated several possible new designs.

Guidelines

There will always be trade-offs, but keep these general principles or goals in mind as you sketch the new process:

Principle	Explanation
Speed	In general, the faster something can go, the more efficient the process.
Quality	Without quality you will lose customers.
Efficiency	Minimum rework and minimum cost are important building blocks of efficiency.
Simplified processes	Use the minimum number of interfaces and activities needed to achieve outputs.
Cross-functionality (systems orientation)	It is important to look at the entire system and entire process. Use a process versus a functional perspective. Functions and staff departments should be minimized and maintain only key expertise.
Proximity of customers to suppliers	It is often important to jointly develop products or services. A supplier may have a person permanently assigned to one customer at the customer's site.
Minimum layer of management	An organization does not need layers and layers of management working on a process. This is not efficient.
Minimum bureaucracy	Activities checking or counting the work of others should be questioned and eliminated (e.g., quality inspection, etc.).
Maximum clarity	There should be few, if any, overlapping responsibilities and fuzzy responsibilities. Clear expectations and goals are critical.
Parallel processing	Many activities can be done at the same time.
Add value	Would the customer pay for these steps if she knew they did not need to be performed? Eliminate activities that fail to add value or contribute to the objectives.

Principle	Explanation
Clear authority/account-ability/decision making	Clarify who has the authority to make certain decisions and who is accountable for the output. Decision making should be passed as far down in the organization as possible. When the process uses teams, there should be a clearly identified team leader who has the authority to manage the team.
Single point of contact	• Do people in the process have a single point of contact? • Do customers and suppliers have a single point of contact? • Do people know who to contact to get specific issues resolved? • How can we use technology to streamline the process even further?
Enhanced technology	Information technology is often a major element in fundamental redesign efforts. An information systems expert can be of tremendous help. For example, a particular organization has multiple databases running on multiple servers. Each of these servers contains a series of reports generated by a certain function (e.g., Finance, quality, etc.). With the right software, a person sitting at a desk can access almost any type of data. The program automatically links to the other servers, grabs the reports the person needs, and sends them to his or her computer. The person can also specify exactly when the report should arrive.
Integration with other systems	How will this new design affect the financial measuring system or the human resource systems?

Before you start

1. Review what your customers want.
2. Refresh yourself on how to chart processes (Chapter 3).

What to do

Steps	Suggested Questions & Approaches
1. Sketch the new process.	Draw a new process map from scratch. Keep the guidelines in mind.
2. Describe the critical outputs.	Start with what the customer(s) want and work backward.
3. Add the activities that must occur, their sequence, and where they occur.	Creat a new process map either by using computer software (e.g., activity-based, program management, flowcharting) or by drawing it manually.
4. Identify the accomplishments/outputs throughout the process and add performance criteria.	For example, a completed quotation is a key accomplishment within the process. Quotations will be 100 percent accurate and sent to customers within four hours of receiving their application.
5. Chart the flow of information. Show where information will be used and what type of information will be used.	For example, the new process map will show that to process a quotation within four hours, all information needed will be available "on-line."
6. Chart the use of technology. Show where technology will be used and what type of technology will be used.	For example, the new process map will show that to process a quotation within four hours, each performer will have a desktop computer that can access the main databases.
7. Check the design against the principles of redesign.	See Guidelines.

Determine How the Current Financial System Needs to Change to Support the New Design

Purpose of this procedure

This procedure helps you determine how the new design will affect the financial system—specifically, what in the financial system will need to change in order to be compatible with the newly designed process. Since much of the human behavior in an organization is based on what is measured and rewarded, it is important to understand whether or not the financial system must be redesigned to reinforce the new process.

When to use this procedure

Use this procedure

- In all fundamental redesigns. Understanding the impact on the financial system is critical. More likely than not, the financial system will need to change to accommodate the new process.

- If you need to assign costs to each of the activities and outputs.

What to do

Steps	Suggested Questions & Approaches
1. Define the behaviors the new process needs to reinforce.	Have the team identify what behaviors need to be tracked and rewarded to produce the desired results.
2. Identify what results need to be tracked.	
3. Compare what the new design requires with what the current financial system rewards and tracks.	Work closely with your Finance expert or the Finance department to ensure that the right behaviors will be reinforced.
4. Identify what changes need to be made to the financial system.	• Are we tracking the right costs?
5. Put the recommended changes on your commitment list.	See Procedure 4.16.

Example

In one particular organization, the key metrics tracked by Finance were performance to sales forecast, performance to budget, and overall profitability. These were the key topics of discussion at operations reviews and other senior executive staff meetings. The organization, however, had a major problem in developing new products.

The organization had sponsored a team to look at improving the new product development process. The team realized no measures were focused on new product development and that there were no process measures. They recommended that each operation also report the percentage of sales from products introduced in the last two years, performance to schedule of each new product development program, cost of delay, and the number of current development programs. The team also created cycle time measures for the five key subprocesses of the new product development process. This helped the team and executive management understand how much time was spent at each of the subprocesses relative to the value of the process.

Procedure 4.13	**Determine How the Current Human Resources System Needs to Change to Support the New Design**

Purpose of this procedure

This procedure will help you determine what in the human resource system will need to change to be compatible with the newly designed process.

When to use this procedure

Use this procedure

- In both incremental and fundamental redesign.
- After you have sketched or charted the new design.

Guidelines

Determine what, if anything, must change in how the human resource system

- Measures, evaluates, and manages performance.
- Rewards individuals or teams.
- Recruits and selects individuals.
- Trains and develops individuals.

What to do

Steps	Suggested Questions & Approaches
1. Confirm that the performance management system supports the new design.	
2. Identify what parts of the compensation system do or do not support the new design.	
3. Identify what parts of the training system do or do not support the new design.	
4. Identify what overall work force skills need to change.	• Does our work force have the skills to support the new design?
5. Identify what general HR practices need to change.	• Can we implement the new design with our current HR practices?
6. Identify how HR information systems can be used to reinforce the new design.	
7. Put your recommended changes on your commitment list.	See Procedure 4.16.

Example

A couple of years prior to the redesign effort, the organization implemented a performance management system. This system was the first experience that this organization had with formally managing performance. Managers needed to complete several pages of documentation manually each time they evaluated performance. Each manager would evaluate his or her subordinates.

A few years later, the redesign team recommended a new process for developing new products. One of the key variables in this new process was that individual contributors could work on up to five different development projects a year, each with a different team leader. Furthermore, goals specified in the performance management plan would often change quarterly or monthly. The performance managment system was not designed for a fast-paced, ever-changing environment. Because it was so cumbersome, managers and project leaders did only what was necessary; they did not use the system to truly help improve performance. Furthermore, the system did not capture the reality that more than one manager might have input into a performer's evaluation.

The redesign team worked with human resources staff to streamline and simplify the performance management system so that it was in greater alignment with the newly designed new-product-development process.

Evaluate the New Design

Purpose of this procedure

Use this procedure to determine if the new design will satisfy the customer's requirements, meet effectiveness criteria, and adhere to good design principles. The purpose of this procedure is to confirm that the redesign you propose is the best way to close the performance gap.

When to use this procedure

Use this procedure after the team has generated a possible new design.

Follow these steps to evaluate the new design:

- Determine all costs associated with the redesign effort. Think of costs not only in terms of dollars, but also in terms of time, potential disruptions, impact on quality, and so on.

- Determine all of the benefits associated with the redesign effort. Think in terms of cycle time, quality improvement, customer satisfaction, and so on.

- Quantify costs and benefits in financial terms wherever you can.

- Compare costs and benefits. Describe specifically why the benefits outweigh the costs.

- Perform a "reality check"—determine if the evaluation makes sense.

Before you start

Assemble the information you gathered, including success factors (Procedure 3.10), details on what customers want (Procedure 4.1), a sketch or map of the new process (Procedure 4.11), and how financial and human resource systems will be affected (Procedures 4.12 and 4.13).

What to do

Steps	Suggested Questions & Approaches
1. Compare the proposed design to the performance criteria the critical business issue demands.	
2. Complete a cost-versus-benefit chart to capture the nonfinancial benefits and costs.	See the example.
3. Determine the cost-to-benefit ratios of the new design.	Include implementation costs. See Guidelines.
4. Based on your answers to steps 1–3, determine if the design works.	

Example

A completed cost-versus-benefit chart might look something like this:

Financial Benefits	Nonfinancial Benefits	Financial Costs	Nonfinancial Costs
For example, had we introduced the X95 on time to win the design, we would have made an additional $1 million in revenue over the life of that product.	We would become recognized as a leader in new products.	Implementation will cost approximately $5 million. This includes new equipment, hardware, and training.	Our entire operations will change.
We've calculated that for this division, the cost of delaying introduction of a product by one week is $300,000. These could be dollars straight into our pocket.	Our operations would be more effective and efficient.	Outside consultation will cost approximately $500,000.	People will need to redefine their jobs.
We can command a higher average selling price.	The more profitable and successful we are, the more we can pay our employees.		Stress will be an issue as we move to the new design. The organization will need to restructure.

| Procedure 4.15 | **Design the Organization Chart** |

Purpose of this procedure

The purpose of this procedure is to allow you to determine the effect of the new design on interdepartmental reporting and relationships and to help you design new reporting structures and organizational structures.

When to use this procedure

Use this procedure after the team has determined the cost-to-benefit ratio of the new design.

Terms you may not know

Organization chart   A chart that shows how and on what basis the organization as a whole groups its tasks (e.g., by products, technology, market segments, processes, functions), as well as reporting relationships.

Guidelines

In the following chart are other principles to keep in mind while determining the organizational structure.

Principle	Explanation
Process-based structures	Organize the structure around processes, not functions. Each process should yield a product or service to a customer.
Process owners	A manager or team should be the "owner" of a core cross-functional process. These individuals will be responsible and accountable for the output of the process.
Teams	Use multidisciplinary, cross-functional teams, or teams with members that have different areas of expertise, to run each process. Each team should have a clearly identified team leader, who has the authority to manage the team.
Accountability/Authority	Make sure that accountability and authority are clear. A manager or team should be accountable for a specified output. Teams should have clearly identified leaders. Teams must have the authority and information needed to achieve the goals for which they are held accountable.
Results	Think of these process owners reporting to a Board of Directors. The Board focuses on results, not day-to-day operations.
Specific targets	Each process should have specific performance objectives that are closely tied to customer satisfaction.

What to do

1. Identify the function (specifically, the department head or senior manager) the process owners report to.

2. Assign accountability and authority for each team to the team leader most capable of managing the team.

3. Set performance objectives for the process. See Procedure 4.1.

4. Identify needed changes in reporting structures and departmental relationships and add them to your commitment list. See Procedure 4.16.

| Procedure 4.16 | ### Prepare for Executive and Steering Committee Presentations |

Purpose of this procedure

It is now time to pull together all the work the redesign team has accomplished and to show management that the redesign is worth implementing. This procedure will help you to clearly outline the entire redesign effort, describe why it is being done, list all the foreseeable implications of the project, and demonstrate how it will improve the organization's performance.

All redesign efforts, from the smallest process-improvement project to the largest organizational overhaul, require approval at some level and some willingness from the people in the organization to "buy into" the plan. These are obtained by presenting the redesign position paper, summary findings, and new design to the organization's executives and the steering committee.

This procedure focuses on creating the recommendations on which executive management will decide. The decision can go two ways:

- Executive management gives the go-ahead to implement the new process as described in the recommendations from the redesign team.

- Executive management requests more data or a different design.

When to use this procedure

Use this procedure

- For incremental redesign projects if the decision to close the gap needs to be made at the executive level (e.g., if it involves a significant capital investment).

- For incremental redesign projects that do not need executive approval, you can adapt this procedure to best address your audience.

- For all fundamental redesign projects. Up to this point the new design has existed only on paper. Not until top management understands its ramifications, resources the effort, and facilitates the implementation will the design achieve its purpose.

Guidelines

The team must demonstrate that the new design will better serve customers, streamline the organization, and increase the organization's ability to perform. Management must be convinced that the new design will close the performance gap and that the benefits will outweigh the costs.

In a fundamental redesign project, the top executive (usually the CEO) needs to be involved. He or she will be able to help the team present its findings so that top management and the steering committee will clearly understand the trade-offs. Top management usually likes to see information that is clear and simple to understand and which includes how much the new process will cost in both financial and nonfinancial terms.

Use both quantitative and qualitative criteria to substantiate your recommendations. Try to maintain a balance in the amount of information you provide: explain how you calculated the numbers, but do not include so much information that it takes months and months to analyze it.

A cost-versus-benefit analysis is a basic business tool; it is an important piece of information in any business decision. The length of your analysis will depend on the number of different costs and the number of possible benefits, as well as on how much detail management needs before they feel comfortable.

Develop a format for presenting your data. Keep your presentation focused and concise, yet comprehensive in its coverage. Here's one way you might organize your presentation:

1. Summarize the position paper.
2. Summarize the current system paper or presentation.
3. Describe the current gaps and their impact on customers.
4. Summarize the new design. Include
   - A cost-versus-benefit analysis.
   - Your new organization chart.
5. Describe what it will take to implement the new design.

Send a copy of the presentation ahead of time to the executive group that will make the decision.

For incremental redesign, you may want to follow a similar presentation format. Recognize, however, that the gap you are trying to close is smaller and that the change required is probably not as large as in fundamental redesign. It may or may not require executive approval. Therefore, your presentation should be adapted to your audience and to the level of change required. You may want to focus on presenting the following:

- The existing process.
- The gap analysis (use your gap analysis worksheet).
- The alternatives and the cost-benefit trade-off.
- You or your team's recommendation (the new process).

What to do

Steps	Suggested Questions & Approaches
1. Review Procedure 3.12.	
2. Prepare a list of management commitments needed to implement the new design.	The decision-making body must commit themselves not only to supporting the effort, but also to actively involving themselves in its implementation.
3. Send a copy of the presentation ahead of time to the group that will make the decision.	
4. Present the report.	Have the entire team there to answer questions as needed.
5. Ask for management commitment to implement the new design.	Refer to your commitment list.

CHAPTER 5

Overcoming Barriers to Implementation

Purpose of this chapter

If your team has done everything well, you will by now have secured executive support and involvement, devised a workable communication strategy, and designed a new process that will close the performance gap. To this point, however, the new process has existed only on paper. Now it is time for "the rubber to hit the road." Employees are going to have to change their behavior. Rules are going to change. Power will be redistributed and relationships reconfigured.

The purpose of this chapter is to provide you with a few basic principles to keep in mind during implementation. It is difficult to provide exact, step-by-step guidelines. Implementations vary from company to company and are dependent on many different variables, such as executive commitment and involvement. The previous chapters described most of the actual tools and procedures you will use. Your success at implementation will largely depend on how much work you have done up front. The key is to work from a plan or road map.

Throughout the project, you have tried to be sensitive to the effect of human behavior on redesign efforts. Implementing the new process is the most critical and difficult step of any redesign effort, and you will soon see that it is the people in the organization who will make or break the change.

Managment must also help keep people focused and pulling in the same direction. The sponsor, team leader, and process owner must have the necessary authority to create a focus for people's efforts. You need to avoid having many teams reinventing what the redesign team has already done, working in opposite directions, or working on similar issues without knowing it. Employee teams must have clear charters and goals that all work toward the same end.

You'll often find that some managers do not share the redesign team's perception of the competitive business environment. Sometimes they are in a state of denial, unable to recognize the need for change. The organization as a whole, however, must move forward. Remember that change tends to upset people. They are frequently afraid to let go of old, familiar ways of doing things. They dislike the ambiguity that surrounds a new process and will work to minimize the personal risks that come with change.

How is this chapter organized?

To determine:	Follow this procedure:
How to implement the new design	Procedure 5.1—Create the Implementation Plan
What problems you might encounter	Procedure 5.2—Overcome "Real World" Barriers

Results

If you follow the recommendations and procedures listed in this chapter, you should achieve the following results:

- Institutionalization of a new core cross-functional process that closes the performance gap. If you link the new process to the financial and human resource systems, impacting how performance is measured and how people are evaluated and rewarded in such a way as to reinforce the goals of the new process, your chances of success are much higher.

- A clear indication (e.g., costs reduced by 25 percent) of whether or not the reason for redesigning a core cross-functional process was valid.

- A clear indication of whether the team closed the performance gap.

For More Information

Bridges, W. *Managing Transitions*. Reading, Mass.: Addison-Wesley, 1991.

Daniels, W. R. *Group Power I: A Manager's Guide to Using Task Force Meetings*. San Diego: Pfeiffer, 1986.

Daniels, W. R. *Group Power II: A Manager's Guide to Conducting Regular Meetings*. San Diego: Pfeiffer, 1990.

Davenport, T. H. *Process Innovation—Reengineering Work through Information Technology*. Boston, Mass.: Harvard Business School Press, 1993.

Eisenhardt, K. "Speed and Strategic Choice: How Managers Accelerate Decision Making." *California Management Review*, 1990, *32* (Spring), 39–54.

Gabarro, J. J. *The Dynamics of Taking Charge*. Boston, Mass: Harvard Business School Press, 1987.

Hammer, M. and Champy, J. *Reengineering the Corporation*. New York: HarperCollins, 1993.

Morris, D. and Brandon, J. *Reengineering Your Business*. New York: McGraw-Hill, 1993.

Phillips, D. *Lincoln on Leadership*. New York: Warner Books, 1992.

Rummler, G. A. and Brache, A. P. *Improving Performance*. San Francisco: Jossey-Bass, 1991.

Ryan, K. D. and Oestreich, D. K. *Driving Fear Out of the Workplace*. San Francisco: Jossey-Bass, 1991.

Schaffer, R. H. and Thomson, H. A. "Successful Change Programs Begin with Results." *Harvard Business Review* (January–February 1992): 80–89.

Wurman, R. S. *Information Anxiety*. New York: Doubleday, 1989.

| Procedure 5.1 | **Create the Implementation Plan** |

Purpose of this procedure

This procedure will help you develop an implementation road map and implementation action plans. It will also help you select appropriate teams or individuals to complete implementation actions.

When to use this procedure

Use this procedure:

- For all redesign projects.
- Before giving the executive presentation.
- When you need a methodology to help manage the implementation of the project or action items.

Terms you may not know

Gantt chart   A specific project planning technique.

Pilot   A test run of the new process. The process may be modified depending on the pilot's success.

Guidelines

Use Gantt charts or project-planning software to determine what has to occur and in what sequence. These tools will also help you to determine what resources are needed and to set target completion dates. This phase of redesign is similar to managing any large-scale project. Your team might solicit the help of an expert in project planning to help with your project plan and to help manage the implementation. Furthermore, your executive sponsor should be highly involved in this phase of the redesign.

The redesign team and the top manager must clearly communicate to all the people involved why the new process is being implemented. The top manager must convey a new vision for the organization and articulate that the current process is not being redesigned because the organization *wants* to change, but because it *must* change in order to survive.

In some cases, usually fundamental redesigns, you will need to pilot the new process to make sure that it works properly and to eliminate any bugs. A pilot run of the new process can also help build support for the change. The pilot can take anywhere from two to twelve months, depending on the significance of the change, the culture of the organization, and the level of executive support.

Keep the following principles in mind as you begin to create your implementation road map.

Managing the shift. Develop a methodology to allow the organization to "cut over" to the new process. As it begins to implement the new design, the organization will most likely perform some parallel tasks between the old and new process. The most important consideration here is to make sure that outputs necessary to making the new process work get accomplished in one way or another during the transition.

Communication. Strive to have open, honest, two-way communication. People need to know what is not working, and they need to be able to openly share their ideas without fear. Listen to all issues raised regarding the performance of the pilot. This is the most critical factor in the entire re-design effort—if you fail here, you will most likely fail altogether. The less ambiguity there is about the redesign the better. Set up meetings where managers and other employees can talk to the redesign team or the executive leading the effort to discuss anything on their mind.

Small wins. Make sure people experience small wins along the way. Develop milestones by which people can tell how they are doing. Build these small indicators of success into the implementation plan. Achieving small successes along the way is critical to maintaining people's faith in eventual overall success. Celebrate the small victories along the way.

Employee involvement. Keep in mind that the employees are making the process work, not the redesign team. Make it clear that you expect employees to take the initiative to help improve and facilitate the implementation. Make sure your team doesn't come across as aloof "experts" or "saviors." A successful implementation depends more on the people who have to change their behaviors than on anyone else.

Working with Human Resources. Work closely with Human Resources to set up training, define new roles and responsibilities, develop job aids, change reward and incentive systems, and help people learn new skills. If your organization has internal consultants, use them to help with the change process. Develop basic skills training programs if necessary. Learn from the pilot how to best teach people the new skills and behaviors they need to function in the new process. As the pilot gets under way and you are helping to improve performance, determine what works most efficiently.

Working with Finance. Work closely with Finance to develop metrics and tracking systems that reinforce the change effort.

Integrating the implementation road map into day-to-day operations. There are three easy and practical vehicles managers can use to help you integrate your efforts into the organization's day-to-day activities:

- Staff meetings. Some managers will prefer to use the staff meeting to discuss required actions, monitor their completion, and generally manage their participation in the transition.

- Operations reviews. Other managers will prefer to track their staff's progress in completing required action plans in monthly reviews.

- Written or formal communications. Many managers will use these forums to communicate to a large population how the redesign project is progressing on a continuing basis.

What to do

Steps	Suggested Questions & Approaches
1. Develop an overall implementation road map.	Use a Gantt chart or project-planning software. This step may include choosing a pilot site or planning to run the pilot at one site and then "fan it out" to the rest of the organization. See Guidelines.
2. Tie the road map to the overall communication plan developed in Chapter 2.	Communication is especially vital during implementation. Make sure that the entire organization knows what is happening and has a vehicle for communicating what they learn to the redesign team. See Guidelines.
3. Develop specific action plans.	
4. Develop a mechanism to manage the implementation of the action.	The organization needs a mechanism to determine whether action items are complete. The redesign team can hold status review meetings where actions are reviewed for completion. You can also integrate status review meetings into regular staff meetings of the executive team (this is often more powerful). If the executive team does not have staff meetings, this would give them a good opportunity to get together to review progress on the road map. The signal this would send is "We are all in this together." See Guidelines.

Example   A completed Gantt chart may look something like this:

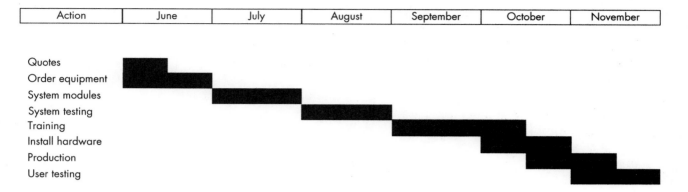

Action	June	July	August	September	October	November

Quotes
Order equipment
System modules
System testing
Training
Install hardware
Production
User testing

Overcome "Real World" Barriers

Purpose of this procedure

In redesigning a process there are certain "real world" barriers that will arise. The purpose of this procedure is to highlight the major and consistently arising barriers and show how you can overcome them.

When to use this procedure

Use this procedure

- If you are having difficulty with any portion of the redesign implementation.

- If you find that the redesign team you are working with is not following the procedures mentioned in this book.

- If you are interested in learning about some of the implementation issues that have arisen in other companies.

Guidelines

Follow the guidelines in the chart on the next four pages. This list of issues is only a sampling of the most commonly found barriers to redesign. Every organization will face its own specific barriers and will need to recognize and address them. In most cases you will not be able to address these barriers alone. Work closely with your sponsor.

Issue	How to Address for Incremental Redesign	How to Address for Fundamental Redesign
Lack of Management Support		
Executives and managers do not know how to do an incremental redesign or what it requires.	Your response will be different depending on who is sponsoring the effort. In a cross-functional redesign it is better if the sponsor has full authority over the functional groups.	
Executives and managers have no incentive or motivation to do an incremental redesign.	Do an analysis of the system to find out why.	
There are environmental factors that keep executives and managers from performing a true incremental redesign.	Determine what these factors are and if they can be overcome.	
Fundamental change is necessary, but the executive staff thinks the problem can be solved incrementally.	The team may begin the project as an incremental redesign, and as the team gathers performance data it may become clear to the executive staff that fundamental change is necessary.	As it becomes clear that fundamental change is necessary, use the data collected to go to senior management and recharter the team. The top manager may see the significance of the issue and involve him/herself in the project. If not, continue with the incremental redesign and document all achievements.
Executives and managers do not know how to do a fundamental redesign or what it requires.		Trace the source of the request: Who originally sponsored the team? Where is he or she in the organization? How much authority does he or she have? If a general manager sponsors and his staff doesn't know redesign, educate the staff. If lower-level person sponsors, determine the level of executive support.
Executives and managers have no incentive or motivation to do a fundamental redesign.		Find out why the original sponsor started the project or asked you to help. What is she noticing that makes her think the business has to improve, and why?
The top manager has no time to devote to the redesign effort.	This may be OK as long as she stays informed.	If the top manager is not willing to devote the necessary time to the project, attempt first to educate him or your sponsor to the importance of his involvement first. If you get no response, the success of a fundamental redesign is in grave danger. Consider not pursuing the project.

	Lack of Sufficient Expectations	
Issue	**How to Address for Incremental Redesign**	**How to Address for Fundamental Redesign**
The performance target is set very low.	Ask why it's so low and can it be set higher?	Ask why it's so low and can it be set higher? It is critical to have an ambitious goal.
The redesign is led by average performers or performers several layers down in the organization.	This may be OK because there is less organizational visibility and the projects tend to be smaller in nature.	Get some "stars" to join the team. Have them present to the team and work with you as much as they can. The organization is watching and wondering if its best people will be working on the project? If so, they will regard it as a serious effort.
No one is taking responsibility for the change effort.	Ask where the sponsorship came from and how committed they are? Raise the issue.	Ask where the sponsorship came from and how committed they are? Raise the issue.
People don't understand redesign. They think it would be a nice thing to try.	Educate them through executive summaries, articles, presentations, consultants.	Educate them through executive summaries, articles, presentations, consultants.
There is resistance by managers.	Determine the cause of the resistance. Work with managers so they will work with you or at least not set roadblocks, even if they disagree with the redesign.	Determine the cause of the resistance. Work with the sponsor and the top executive to address any resistance.
There is resistance by top management.	The redesign may not affect them. If it does, work with your sponsor to clarify their expectations.	Let your sponsor or the top executive handle this.
No one knows why this has to be done.	Communicate the reason why this is important to do.	Communicate the reason why this must be done. It's not something that is just a nice improvement, it's a must.
There are factors outside the top executive's control that are influencing the process.	Determine what they are and if they will influence your redesign. If so, talk it through with the executive or your sponsor.	Determine what they are and if they will influence your redesign. If so, talk it through with the executive or your sponsor.

	Lack of Appropriate Emphasis	
Issue	How to Address for Incremental Redesign	How to Address for Fundamental Redesign
No one has any time. Everyone is fighting fires.	Depending on the performance gap, this may be OK (again, because the effort may be much smaller).	You need a full-time team. And you need a lot of involvement from the top executive. Convince your sponsor.
There are too many programs going on and this is just number 20 of 30.	Combine the programs into one major change effort if possible. Or take the focus away from other programs. Or kill some programs.	Combine the programs into one major change effort if possible. Or take the focus away from other programs. Or kill some programs.
There are no resources available for this effort. Resources are limited, especially money.	Factor this in as one of your constraints when you are looking at alternatives.	Fundamental redesign will cost some money. The top executive or the sponsor will have to deal with this issue.
The culture is used to thinking tactically using Band-Aids versus strategically.	Educate people on the need to take a systematic, data-driven, analytic approach. Mention that you understand their fears of analysis paralysis and you will not fall into that trap.	Educate people on the need to take a systematic, data-driven, analytic approach. Mention that you understand their fears of analysis paralysis and you will not fall into that trap. Show them the overall redesign game plan.
The organization likes to solve problems by chartering a team for everything. Efforts are not focused. Projects have no clear beginning and ending.	Determine what teams are working on and their focus. Eliminate some teams, combine other teams. Teach the organization how to charter a team, set boundaries, clarify authority, etc.	Determine what teams are working on and their focus. Eliminate some teams, combine other teams. Redesign is usually done by one team and possibly some focused subteams. Teach the organization how to charter a team, set boundaries, clarify authority, etc.
There are several teams working on different elements of the process.	Make sure the teams communicate and update each other regularly.	Find a way to coordinate all redesign activities. Create a steering committee that has full authority. Teams working on different elements of the same problem become subteams. You can also combine teams into one team.

(continued on next page)

Issue	How to Address for Incremental Redesign	How to Address for Fundamental Redesign
The organization does not have the necessary data available to construct a current process map (time and cost data for process steps) and is unable to get it.	Gather the data from task performers and "guesstimate." You need a current process map with performance data in order to begin. Without this map you will not really know what to improve, it will be difficult to set targets, the organization will never get an understanding of the entire process/system, and you will run the risk of the entire redesign project failing.	Gather the data from task performers and "guesstimate." You need a current process map with performance data in order to begin. Without this map you will not really know what to improve, it will be difficult to set targets, the organization will never get an understanding of the entire process/system, and you will run the risk of the entire redesign project failing.

What to do

Steps	Suggested Questions & Approaches
1. Define and categorize the issues you encountered.	Recognize that each issue may fall under more than one category. 1. Lack of management support 2. Lack of sufficient expectations
2. Follow the appropriate procedure.	3. Lack of appropriate emphasis See Guidelines.

SECTION THREE

PROCESS REDESIGN IN ACTION

Overview

What is this section about?

No two companies encounter exactly the same situations, and no two companies address similar problems in exactly the same way. Therefore, each process redesign project must be a highly creative and unique endeavor. There is no one "right" way to redesign a business process. The procedures you read about in Section Two are meant only to provide you with a set of tools—it is up to you to use them as you see fit. The "right" way to use them is whichever way meets your objective. If your redesign closes the performance gap, improves the operations of the company, and satisfies the customer in the most cost-effective and efficient manner possible, then you will have discovered the "right" way to redesign.

However, even though each redesign effort is like an individual work of art, it is often useful to study the technique of other artists. This section provides you with two case studies of complete cross-functional redesign efforts. These examples are meant to give you ideas and to stimulate your imagination. Since redesign can take anywhere from a few weeks to a few years, the examples are necessarily condensed. There should be enough detail, however, to give you valuable additional insight on how to redesign a cross-functional process.

How this section is organized?

This section is split into two chapters, each examining a different type of redesign process. Chapter 6 describes the fundamental redesign of "Alpha" Corporation's new-product-development process, and Chapter 7 the incremental redesign of "Beta" Corporation's order-to-collection process.

Case Study 1—Fundamental redesign

Alpha Corporation, a Fortune 1000 manufacturer, was having problems developing new products. They had no formal new-product-development process, so they decided to begin with a "blank piece of paper." After investigating their current, informal process, they developed a phased new-product-development process. A project such as this falls near the fundamental end of the redesign continuum (versus the incremental end). The new design addressed Alpha's need for more discipline in the way they develop new products. They could have pursued even more fundamental change by designing a new-product-development process with only one "go/no go" gate, but the organization was not ready for this type of change.

Case Study 2—Incremental redesign

Beta Corporation is a small supplier of point-of-sale material. They needed to reduce their costs, so they decided to look at their entire order-to-collection process. They first completed a detailed analysis of the process and then redesigned their current system. Although a project such as this falls closer to the incremental end of the redesign continuum, the potential impact of this change is great.

CHAPTER 6

Speeding Up High-Tech Product Development: Case Study of Fundamental Redesign

Overview

Alpha Corporation is a large high-technology manufacturing organization with operations around the world. The company was performing fairly well, but it was concerned about its ability to keep pace with the rapidly changing high-technology industry. Product life cycles were constantly getting shorter and there was a need for more and more new products. Metrics such as sales from products introduced in the last three years became increasingly important. Cycle time management and competition based on time had become the industry's rallying cry. New-product-development cycle time became a major strategic imperative.

The redesign team

The CEO and top management staff at Alpha recognized the need to improve their new-product-development process. They chartered a team led by Strategic Planning to develop a new process, starting with product conception, progressing to high-volume production, and ending with market release. The team was cross-functional in nature, with membership from Marketing, Engineering, Finance, Manufacturing, Human Resources, and Strategic Planning. The executive staff stayed in close contact with the redesign team, and the CEO was essentially the sponsor of the effort.

The charter

It did not take the team long to recognize there were problems. They did not have to spend hundreds of hours drawing a detailed map of how new products were currently developed in each division. Instead, they took a high-level view of the process, and they quickly understood the issues:

- There was no formal new-product-development process.
- There was no discipline in the system.
- People were not held accountable.
- Departments and groups battled each other.
- What process there was was fragmented.
- Research threw new-product ideas over the wall to Marketing, who threw them to Manufacturing.

The team's charter was clear—fix the problem. Top management set the expectations—they were behind this effort 100 percent, and a new process *would* be implemented. The team was to determine the best possible process.

Communication

Everyone knew there was a team looking at a new-product-development process that would be implemented across the entire organization. The team had an "open door policy." If people were concerned or had questions, they could schedule time with any of the team members to get answers to their questions. A massive, company-wide communication effort was planned for the duration of the redesign project.

Interviews

The team met and generated a list of people they wanted to talk to to get a better understanding of the problem. Exhibit A summarizes what they discussed.

Exhibit A: Critical Issue Worksheet

Q: What are the specific results or outputs that are not being achieved?

A: New products make up a small portion of overall sales. Not enough new products are released in a timely manner. The company has missed market windows, missed "design ins."

Q: How do you know this is a problem? Are there any specific metrics that indicate this is a problem?

A: A recent customer survey cited new product delivery as a major issue, and competitor analyses have shown that others are faster at delivering new products. Others have had their products designed into our customers' products.

Q: If this were no longer a problem, how would you know? What would be the relevant indicators? How would you know it was solved, specifically?

A: A larger portion of our sales would be from new products. Future customer surveys would indicate that we are better at delivering new products. The time it took us to develop a new product would be greatly reduced. We would win more "design-ins."

Q: What customers were concerned?

A: The survey focused on our top ten customers, but all customers probably have this issue.

Q: What does the customer say he or she wants? Why is this important to the customer?

A: All of our customers find this issue critical. Their customers are asking them to develop new products faster, because the consumer market is changing so quickly.

Q: What do you think our customers expect that they have not said?

A: They expect us to have this issue fixed soon, or they will go elsewhere. Also, they would be willing to pay a premium price if we could supply them quickly.

Q: What do you think would excite our customers?

A: They would be very excited if we had a way to give them different options quickly, ahead of any of their other suppliers; if we could show them how our product addresses several applications; and if we could provide a whole "system."

Q: Who are the customer's customers, and what do they need to be successful?

A: In many cases it is the consumer. For example, our largest customer needs to bring a new product to market every three months to keep up with consumer demand and ahead of his competitors.

(continued on next page)

Exhibit A *(cont.)*

Q: Why is this output important to you?

A: *Our ability to meet our five-year projections is dependent on our ability in developing new products.*

Q: What do you believe would be the impact of closing this gap on our customers and on the organization?

A: *Our customers would be satisfied. We would be able to meet our growth targets.*

Q: Is this critical business issue linked to the strategic plan?

A: *Absolutely.*

Q: What is the best process to redesign to address the critical business issue?

A: *The new-product-development process, starting with creating the concepts and ending with when the product is released for volume manufacturing.*

Q: Will this process have an impact on our customers?

A: *Yes.*

Q: Can this process be redesigned?

A: *With the right kind of management involvement, yes. They have to be serious. We've seen too many attempts at "quick fixes."*

Q: Will redesigning this process affect overall unit performance? How?

A: *Yes—newer products usually command a higher selling price.*

Q: In redesigning this process to close the performance gap, will we need to redesign incrementally or fundamentally?

A: *Don't know.*

Current process sketch	The team next drew a rough sketch of the current process. They identified the major outputs of the process and where they go. They identified the major inputs and where they come from. They drew how the different functions (marketing, design, etc.) convert the input into the output. Their objective was to see the entire system as a series of inputs and outputs, where the output of one function is the input to another. But the team discovered that every business unit developed products in its own way. There was no map that could capture how the entire organization developed products.
Management go-ahead	The team went back to the management committee with their initial findings. The committee confirmed who would sponsor the effort and who should be in the steering committee. They also confirmed what departments and disciplines would be represented on the redesign team. (See Exhibit B.)

Exhibit B: Design Team Charter Worksheet

Critical Business Issue:	Not developing new products fast enough
Process:	New product development (concept to volume mfg.)
Sponsor:	CEO
Steering Committee Members:	CEO's staff
	Top management staff
Redesign Team Members:	Strategic planning manager (team leader)
	Device engineer
	Product engineers (2)
	Information systems technician
	Finance manager
	Performance technologist/HR/training
	Product marketer

Understanding the Current System

The current process

The team began their in-depth analysis of the current process by interviewing people in product development. They found that the current new-product-development process was informal, to say the least. As it turned out, the team did not have to spend much time trying to map the current process, because there was no process. Products were developed on an ad hoc basis—individual engineers and managers simply got together to determine if a particular idea might work. Much time was then spent "selling" the idea upward. There was no formal process, nor were there any formal criteria. The most important variable was how well an individual could convince a manager that something was a good idea. If an executive wanted a product developed, it would be developed. Usually an engineer or a manager would take an idea and translate it into a product. Once the product was somewhat defined, a product champion would appear. This might be a product engineer, a marketer, a manager—almost anyone. This person would then "make the product happen." The probability of the product actually being manufactured depended on the sales skills of the product champion. (While product champions are needed in any organization, they too often become product zealots who try to get their product approved in any way possible.)

The problems

The team delved deeper into the details of this improvised process, discovering a variety of troubling shortfalls and inconsistencies:

- There was almost no process to "harness" the intelligence of the organization.

- There was no review criteria for a group of individuals to use to determine the feasibility of developing a potential new product.

- There was little or no reliance on actual business data (time to break even, sales over the product life cycle, linkage to technology development, etc.). Sometimes market analyses were done thoroughly and sometimes they were mere guesses.

- Each business unit used a separate process to develop new products.

- Products were often developed by a small group in isolation, without consultations with others in the organization.

- Proposed projects were not compared to one another to determine the best use of resources.

- Projects would begin with some funding, but then the funding would often "dry up" and engineers would have to go in search of more resources.

- Customers often wanted systems solutions, but because of its "silo" mentality or functional myopia the organization could not provide them as effectively as possible.

The consequences

The team also researched the consequences of the organization's undisciplined approach:

- The organization wasted a lot of energy and resources.
- A high percentage of its products failed in the market.
- The product portfolio grew at an enormous rate.
- It was difficult to kill bad product ideas.
- Many new products did not add to the profitability of the organization.
- Many new products did not focus on the organization's core competencies.
- The process was not fast.
- The organization had lost focus.
- Customers were not satisfied.

The critical business issue

The team summarized their findings on a chart. (See Exhibit C.) The key issue was that the organization was expending a tremendous amount of energy with little return. This cross-functional team clearly understood the issues, and they decided to move into designing a new process rather quickly. The team agreed that what was needed was a new process that minimizes time to market, meets financial objectives, and hits the market window at the appropriate time to meet the organization's strategic imperatives.

Exhibit C: Current Process Worksheet

Theme	Frequency Heard (rare, some-what rare, sometimes, often)	Populations	Unique?	Comments
Products developed on an ad hoc basis.	often	Engineering Marketing	no	
No formal process.	often	Engineering Marketing	no	
No process to "harness" intelligence.	sometimes	Engineering Marketing	no	
No review criteria.	sometimes	Engineering Marketing Finance	no	
Little or no actual business data used.	sometimes	Engineering Marketing Finance	no	
Projects not compared to each other to determine the best use of resource dollars.	often	Engineering Marketing Finance	no	
Sales from new products a small percentage of overall sales.	often	Engineering Marketing	no	

The current organizational culture

To better understand the source of these problems, the team wanted to learn more about the organization's culture, about which behaviors are valued and how things are celebrated. To help them do this, the team conducted a culture survey. (See Exhibit D.)

Exhibit D: Current Culture Survey

Q: How open is the culture to new ideas?

A: Executives say they are open to new ideas, but people below the executive level don't think this is true.

Q: How much analysis is expected before a group of managers or executives will champion a new idea?

A: Executives and managers say they are willing to champion new ideas, but their behavior indicates that they do not like to take risk. Risk taking is punished.

Q: Are people willing to change?

A: Some executives are, many managers are not, and most engineers and individual contributors are.

Q: Are there certain critical variables that convince people that change is necessary more than other variables do?

A: Business performance; if the CEO is trusted, when top executives communicate openly.

Q: What is the risk tolerance of the culture?

A: Risk taking is often punished.

Q: How conservative is the culture fiscally and elsewhere?

A: Very conservative. Money is not spent unless the return is virtually assured.

Q: How have radically new ideas been introduced, if ever, in the past?

A: There have been very few radically new ideas. Those that have been radical have been sponsored by a few very aggressive managers.

Q: What are the culture's basic assumptions regarding risk, change, analysis, safety, and openness.

A: Risk taking should be avoided; a thorough analysis needs to be done before actions are taken, but there is a fear of analysis paralysis; open, direct, confrontational dialogue should be avoided.

Q: Who are the heroes? What makes them heroes (e.g., inviting change, encouraging innovation, taking risks)?

A: The heroes are the people that don't rock the boat but still help the business perform—the politicians.

Q: What gets celebrated? Innovation?

A: Authentic celebration rarely occurs; there is always the message that "you could have done it better."

(continued on next page)

Exhibit D (cont.)

Q: What are the rites and rituals around conformity?

A: There is strong conformity—don't confront anyone openly, don't ask tough questions in meetings, don't embarrass anyone by asking whether something is complete in an open forum.

Q: Who gets promoted?

A: Politicians.

Q: To get ahead, is it more important to be political and posture or to do what is best for the business and its customers?

A: It's more important to be political, though the "party line" is that the organization is performance-based.

Q: How much time is spent doing activities for activity's sake versus achieving results?

A: A lot. Activities done for activity's sake makes it look like you're doing something. You've got to show results quickly, even if there's not a lot of substance.

Q: What percentage of your decisions do not need approval or a signature from anyone else?

A: Don't know.

Q: How candid can you be about issues?

A: Depends on who you talk to.

Q: What has happened to people who have been direct, open, and completely honest about issues?

A: They are usually put on a slower track. They don't move up as quickly.

Q: Are people measured on results or on completing many activities?

A: Activities.

Q: Is this organization driven by people's obtaining results or by their "looking like" they are obtaining results?

A: A combination of both—looking like you're getting results sure helps.

Q: Do you believe it is easy to get things accomplished, or that there is too much bureaucracy?

A: Too much bureaucracy.

Incentives and rewards

Because the team recognized that the success of their new design will depend largely upon the organization's ability to influence human behavior, they decided to question the Finance and Human Resources managers. They were asked to describe current problems that they would like to see addressed and potential problems with redesigning the process. Their responses are shown in Exhibit E.

Exhibit E: Financial and Human Resource Systems Analysis Survey

1. Metrics currently don't track new product sales very well.

2. We do not have an understanding of how much activities cost.

3. We will need to look closely at how financial metrics reinforce the new design.

4. _____

5. _____

1. Training is not currently focused on improving job performance.

2. Compensation systems will need to be looked at closely—will they reinforce new behaviors?

3. Performance management systems (how we measure performance) may need to be modified.

4. _____

5. _____

Process analysis   The team then decided to sit back and take stock of their efforts. They summarized their investigations and the data they had collected on the worksheets shown in Exhibits F through H.

Exhibit F: Process Analysis Worksheet, Part 1—Understanding the Current System

Have you ...	Yes or No
Sketched the core process?	Informally
Determined the main output(s) of this process?	Yes
Sketched or listed the tasks that make up each activity?	No
Charted the flow of information?	Yes
Charted the use of technology?	Yes
Identified where activities occur?	Yes

Exhibit F: Process Analysis Worksheet, Part 2—Current Performance Data

Activity	Length of Time to Perform the Activity and Achieve the Ouput of the Activity	Resources Needed (People, $, Etc.)	Comments
Defining product concept	Can take years before the concept is translated into a specification	Hard to quantify	
Defining product specification	Usually several weeks	1 engineer 30 person/days	Every engineer creates the preliminary specs his or her own way.
Analyzing the business opportunity	2 days to 6 months		There's no set format for what should be included when analyzing the opportunity.
Building prototype	3–5 weeks	2–3 engineers working full time. Average cost, not including time, is $50,000	Often prototypes must be built 3–4 times because there is insufficient modeling capability.
Launching the product into the market	2–3 weeks	1–2 engineers or marketers working half time	The marketing effort is often behind; no merchandising is available; there's no strategy for target marketing and no roll-out plan.

Overall, the organization calculated that if it introduced a product late it would lose approximately $300,000 per week on average in potential revenue for every week late. In some cases, if "design-ins" were missed, the loss in revenue could be much higher.

Exhibit F: Process Analysis Worksheet, Part 3—Current Success Factors and Roadblocks

What factors are contributing to the success of the current process?	Why?	What causes these factors?
Flexibility	Allows the engineer to adapt quickly.	The need to react quickly to changing demands. Lack of any disciplined approach makes it appear that this is fast.
Empowerment	Project managers feel they can manage their product in any way they want.	Overall thrust in the organization for empowerment.
Dedicated people	People care about the organization and its success.	
Relatively modern equipment	Allows prototypes to be built quickly.	The organization has been willing to fund equipment.
What factors impede the success of the current process?	**Why?**	**What causes these factors?**
Information systems	Investing in systems has been neglected.	Management not understanding the need for systems' and information systems' inability to translate the capabilities into business impacts.
Empowerment	Project managers feel they can manage their product in any way they want.	Overall thrust in the organization for empowerment; poor definition of empowerment; no boundaries.
Lack of discipline in the process	Allows for inefficiency; everybody does it his or her own way.	Current culture and how managers manage the operation.
No common framework	Allows for inefficiency; everybody does it his or her own way.	Current culture and how managers manage the operation.
No joint decision making	Management has never operated as a true staff.	Current culture and how managers manage the operation.

Creating a New Design

**Customer
identification**

The team identified the customers they wanted to focus on and determined their needs (see Exhibit G).

Exhibit G: Customer Needs Worksheet

Who are our current customers?

External = any organization that is external to our company (not part of Alpha) and purchases our products and

services. Internal = our sister divisions.

Who are our future customers?

Mostly the same set, except ZYA and TFP will emerge as leaders in the switch market.

Customers	ABC	XYZ	ZYA	TFP
How profitable?	Good	Somewhat	Very	Very
How much revenue is generated by this customer?	$20 million	$15 million	$10 million	$5 million
What percent of our overall sales goes to this customer?	2%	1.5%	1%	0.5%
Will this customer be strategically important to us? Why?	Yes, strong international presence	Yes, market leader	Yes, high growth	Yes, high growth
Who are this customer's suppliers?	Delta Aeric	Sam	Rigo	Jelco
Who are this customer's customers?	Distributors, Retailers	Distributors	Retailers	Retailers
Strengths?			Technology, speed of execution	Technology, speed of execution
Weaknesses?		Capacity	Size, no deep pockets	Size, R&D
Competitive threats to this customer?	New market entrants	Pricing		

(continued on next page)

Exhibit G *(cont.)*

Customers	ABC	XYZ	ZYA	TFP
Market share in each operation to which we sell our products?	?	33%	10%	5%
Overall financial performance?	Sales of $10 million			
Customer's problems and concerns?	Our capacity	Our delivery		
Customer's growth potential?	Medium	Medium	Strong	Strong

Scope of Redesign

The team then matched what they learned against the criteria for choosing incremental or fundamental redesign. They decided fundamental redesign was necessary (see Exhibit H).

Exhibit H: Worksheet for Choosing Incremental or Fundamental Redesign

Question	Yes or No
Is the level of improvement required considered a paradigm shift?	Yes
To achieve the goal, will the organization need to operate under different assumptions?	Yes
Is the bureaucracy considered overwhelming and stifling?	Yes
Are people operating in silos?	Yes
Are there many problems in the execution of this cross-functional process?	Yes
Even by improving every step in the process, would we not reach our goal?	?
Does the organization's culture need to change?	Yes
To achieve the improvement, will other systems and departments (i.e., HR, Finance) need to change?	Yes
Are we on a "burning platform" (is the business in major trouble)?	No
Is the process fragmented?	Yes

Key process attributes   Before going in and designing specific steps, the team carefully described what should be the key attributes of the new process:

Secure resources. The team stressed that resources for a new-product-development program must be approved before product development begins. After the organization assesses a product's viability in the marketplace, it must commit to developing the product up front. In the past, when times were difficult, the first cost-cutting measures always hit development. Individual product champions would be asked to make do with less (e.g., "You can live another three months without a workstation").

Cross-functional teams. No longer would an individual champion a product by him or herself. A team would be chartered with a specific definition of what they need to accomplish during the process. The team would consist of members from all the different functions: Engineering, Marketing, Quality Assurance, Manufacturing, Product Management, and so on. The team might include other experts or customers as needed. The team would have a clear sponsor who could remove resource roadblocks, connect the team to the sponsoring staff, and act as a coach. The sponsor would have the authority to secure the necessary resources from the appropriate managers. The team would also have a team leader, chosen by the sponsor, whose primary responsibilities would be to choose team members, keep the team on track, and manage the project. The team leader would have the authority to manage the team, but the entire team would be held accountable for its output.

Restructured authority. Authority would be pushed downward. Teams would have the authority to approve what is necessary to bring the project to completion. After management has authorized a new product, there should be no further need for management approval unless there is a deviation from the original proposal.

Customer consultation. A new product would no longer be just the "brainchild" of someone within the company. Each new product would have to be closely linked to a customer need. This would require close, open, and constant communication with the customer. The Quality Function Deployment methodology might be used to translate customer needs. To ensure that the customer is consulted, the process would have certain "gates" (described below) where one of the criteria for passing the product along would be customer acceptance.

Formalized process. The team recognized that ideas might still arise spontaneously, but they stressed that before the company exerted too much effort on a new product idea or the product gathered too much momentum, the product would have to meet specific criteria for marketability, customer expectations, manufacturing, financial potential, sales support, and so on. Throughout the process, from idea to market launch, there would be a series of gates with specific criteria the product must satisfy in order to be moved along. Each of these gates has certain criteria that the cross-functional team must meet. Based on these criteria, a decision would be made at each of these gates on whether the product would go forward, get killed, or be put on hold.

There would be different criteria to satisfy at each different gate. For example, the first gate might require a market analysis; a competitor analysis; linkage to the organization's core competencies; a value-added test; and a clear definition of required technologies, potential customers, relevant financial metrics, and potential strategic implications. Another gate further downstream might require product specifications, a product-development road map or project plan, a prototype design, and customer review and commitment. A gate even further downstream might require manufacturing and quality-control data, selection of test sites, a review of financial metrics and value added, a review of competitive threats, and a market release.

Flexibility. Although the redesign team was proposing the development of a formal process, they recognized the need for flexibility. All gates would be scheduled at the beginning of the process. When all the results (deliverables) for a particular gate were complete, the review process would begin. Therefore, the review process could begin either on a scheduled date or beforehand. Furthermore, depending on the product and its unique requirements, there would be a mechanism to modify pieces of the process if necessary. The amount of documentation required for each new product might be different, depending on the complexity and financial risk of the specific project. Therefore, the documentation requirements would need to be flexible.

Discipline in the system. A product would not be launched until it had passed through all of the gates. No resources would be spent on development until it had passed the first gate. Deliverables would have to be presented and signed-off by an appropriate manager. The management level responsible would depend on how far down the organization wanted to push decision making and accountability. Customer commitments would be pursued only after the product had passed a certain gate. Product teams would be responsible for the quality, accuracy, and comprehensiveness of the data presented at each stage.

Postmortems. After the product had been launched and data was available to gauge the performance of the product, the cross-functional team would get together to determine what worked well and what went wrong. Their findings would be applied to subsequent new-product launches. Managers, too, would be rewarded for learning from their earlier mistakes, sharing their learning, and performing successfully on subsequent launches.

Process steps

After specifying the desired attributes of the new process, the team designed the actual steps in the process. In this case, the steps consisted of a series of review gates and the information necessary at each gate to make a go, no go, or hold decision.

The team concluded that there are essentially five major stages in a new-product-development process:

1. Exploratory phase. The new product idea is first brought to the attention of Marketing.
2. Feasibility phase. The new product idea is investigated for feasibility in the marketplace.
3. Prototype phase. The product is actually developed.
4. Pilot phase. The product is tested.
5. Ramp-up phase. The product is manufactured in volume.

Review gates

The team also recognized the need for review gates. They created six:

1. Product idea review
2. Market review
3. Full authorization review
4. Design and preproduction review
5. Release to manufacturing review
6. Program review

The redesign team then determined several variables that had to be in place for each of these gates. These variables were

- The information that must be present in order to make a go/no go/hold decision.
- The person with the final authority to make the decision at each gate.
- The inputs into each review gate.
- The outputs from each review gate.
- The people—from the core team and elsewhere—who must be present at each review meeting.

For example, at the first review gate (product idea review) the inputs necessary to make a decision are 1) a one-page product business case and 2) a one-page product specification. The product business case would contain data on competitors, customers, potential sales volume, time to break even, development costs, strategic importance, linkage to the core competency, the overall market, potential staffing needs, and the likely market window. The product specification would contain data on product parameters, electrical and physical properties, and so on. The redesign team's intent was to ensure that management would have sufficient data to make a decision on whether to sponsor a team or an individual to take a closer look at each potential market opportunity. At this point that authority would lie with the marketing director. At other review gates, other people would be responsible for making the decision. (When the new process was first implemented, the marketing director pulled together a group of individuals to advise her on what to do given the data. She then made the final decision to sponsor a team.) Therefore, the output of the first review gate, if there is a "go" decision, would be the creation of a cross-functional team to gather more data about the product's market opportunity. The product development team would then create a project plan on how to manage the development project in order to hit a specific market release date.

New process map

The diagram on pages 184–185 is an example of the newly designed new-product-development review process.

Once the paper design was complete the team evaluated this alternative to leaving the status quo and the costs/benefits associated with this design (see Exhibit I).

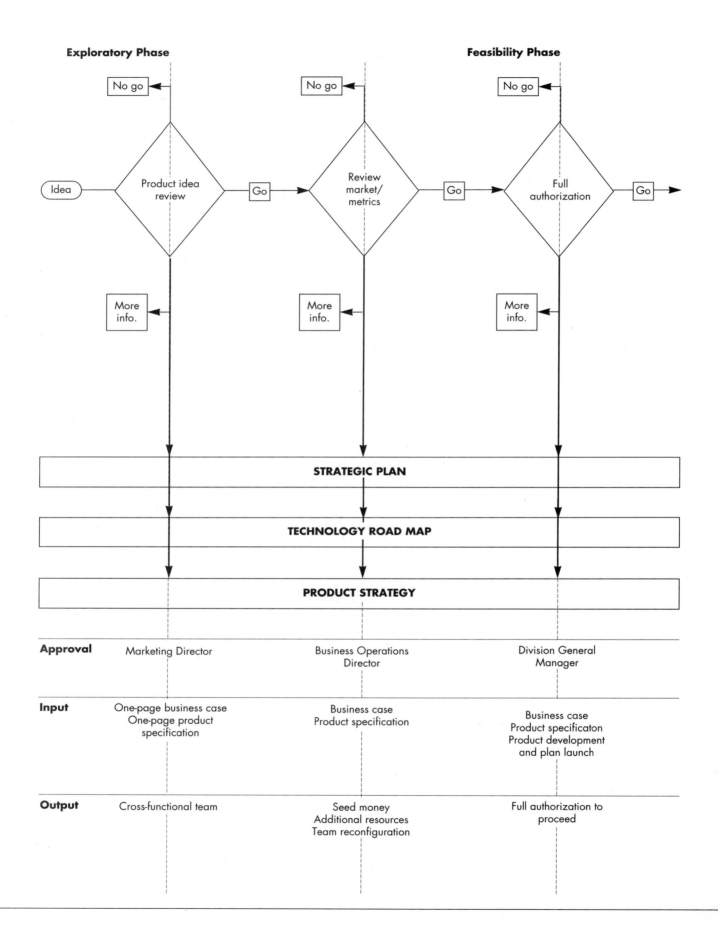

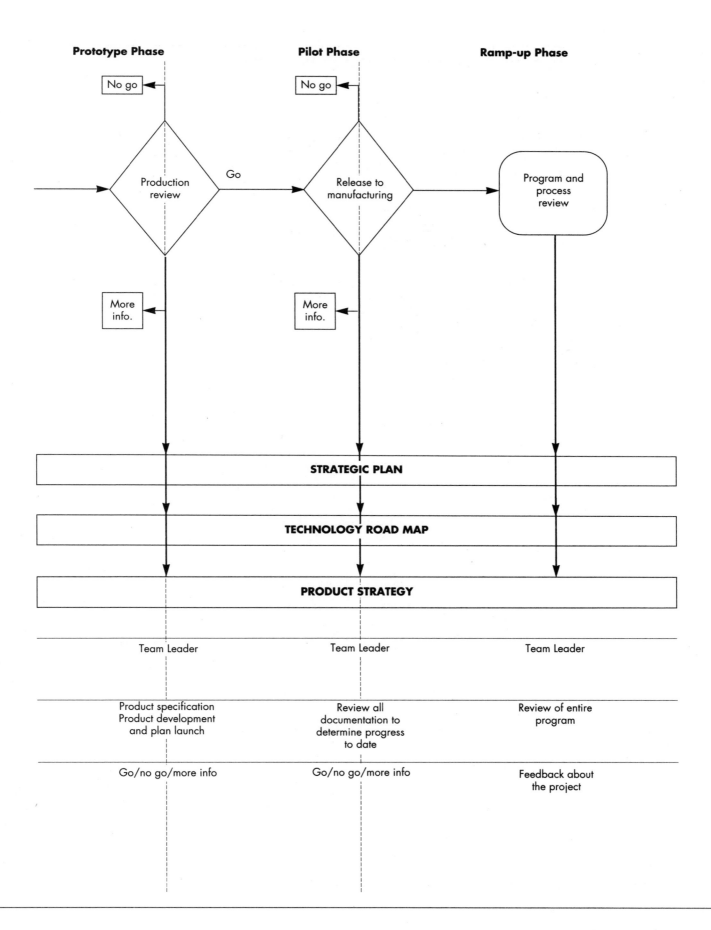

Exhibit I: Accomplishments and Activities Worksheet

Criteria/ Constraints	Alternative		Alternative	
	Review	Process	No Review	Process
	Yes	No	Yes	No
Discipline	✓			
Flexibility		✓	✓	
Speed in developing new products	✓			✓
Reinforcing teamwork	✓			✓
Reduction of silos	✓			✓
Total	4	1	1	3

Implementing the New Design

Management support

It was clear that top management supported the new design. Not only were top managers continuously involved with the redesign team, they also spent many hours advising and working with the team. The top executive was also intimately involved and showed the organization by his actions that implementation of the new process was critical. He clearly stated that he expected the entire organization to use this new process, even though some people disagreed with its methodology. This alone created a clear focus in the organization on what was important.

Communication

After final approval by the sponsor and the steering committee, the next step was to communicate the new process to the entire organization and begin implementation. The design was first worked out on paper and all the deliverables were defined. The information needed for each review step was clearly identified. This clarity allowed the organization to automate all of the information transfers. Engineers then had documents online (e.g., the one-page business case) and could send them to anyone by electronic mail. Furthermore, since there was consistency in the documents used by the organization, comparisons between product opportunities could be made quickly and easily. Communication and the speed of execution were greatly enhanced.

From the beginning the team had an open-door policy. Any individual who wanted to know what was happening along the way could take the initiative to find out. But now, to communicate the new process to the entire organization, it was necessay to hire a consulting firm to train all the individuals in the company in the new methodology. Each person spent half a day listening to presentations from their managers on the importance of the new process. Managers communicated why the new process was important and how it was going to improve the performance of the organization. During these presentations, the floor was open for any type of question, and executives would respond immediately. Everyone spent time in small groups working on sample cases and activities and other exercises to familiarize them with the new process.

Integration and rewards

To better integrate this new process into the overall system, the organization changed its goal-setting process and its appraisal and reward system. This was more a matter of facilitation than it was an ironclad requirement for implementation—top management expected and required people to use the new process. But, by integrating this process into its performance management system and by rewarding people for working in cross-functional teams, sharing their learning, and using the new process, the organization accelerated the acceptance of the new process.

Success factors

Overall, the development and implementation of the new-product-development process was deemed a success. New products were being developed more quickly and the products that were being developed had a greater likelihood of success in the marketplace.

Some of the key success factors of this redesign were

- Strong executive support. The effort was sponsored by the CEO and his top team. Top management indicated that the project was a high priority.

- Executive team focus. There were other change efforts under way, but it was clear to everyone that they were of lesser importance. The redesign of this process was of top priority. The executive team made sure that resources were not stretched so thin that no major strategic change effort could take place.

- Adequate groundwork for change. Time was spent clarifying why this needed to be done. Top management clearly articulated their expectations ahead of time. The top executive wrote a paper explaining his ideas for the organization.

- Constant communication. Open, two-way communication is the cornerstone of any change effort. Executives not only presented what was going to happen, they also facilitated employees' voicing their concern. More importantly, executives tried hard to "walk the talk."

- Emphasis on the strategic plan and core competencies of the organization. The redesign of a new process needs to be closely tied to the organization's overall strategy. It is not meant to alter the strategy. Process redesign answers the question "How can we do things differently?" It does not define what business the company should be in or what it should do. Those questions are properly decided as part of the strategy-making process.

- Adequate resource commitment. The organization was willing to spend the necessary resources to make the change happen. This included purchasing equipment, committing employees' time to the effort, hiring consultants, and so on.

- A small core redesign team and help from experts. This organization used a small cross-functional team to look at the entire process, supplementing their expertise with appropriate experts as needed. This facilitated the adoption of a system view that integrated all of the organization's operations. There were no teams working at cross-purposes.

- Organization-wide commitment. Once the decision was made to design a new process, all executives committed to accepting the design created by the team. There was ample opportunity for discussion up front, but once the decision was made to proceed it was expected that each individual would commit to implementation, even though he or she might not agree with the new design.

CHAPTER 7

Reducing the Cost of Point-of-Purchase Displays: Case Study of Incremental Redesign

Overview

Beta Corporation is a retailer with franchise operations across the United States. One of its marketing responsibilities is to provide national promotional campaigns supported by point-of-purchase (POP) sales support kits for its ten thousand U.S. franchises. While there are twelve national promotions a year, the POP kits are optional—individual stores choose whether or not to buy the kits.

Four Beta departments must work cross-functionally to make the program work:

- Marketing creates the idea and is held accountable for the creative concept.

- Purchasing contracts with vendors to manufacture kit components, to pick and pack the kits, and to ship the kits. It is also held accountable for the cost and quality of the kit.

- Sales and Customer Support market the kits to individual stores and process orders. They are held accountable for order accuracy.

- Accounting bills participating stores and pays contractors. It is held accountable for timely billing and payment, reconciliation, and collections.

The POP kit program is time-critical. No matter what happens with the process inputs (delays in creative conception, artwork, and printing; stock unavailability, and so on), the kits must ship on schedule. Since the media roll-out is set, a late kit would not support the advertising campaign and would have tremendous impact on the franchisee. The POP kit program is also cost-intensive. Delays due to reworking requirements because the product does not meet specifications can sometimes double projected costs.

Purchasing led the redesign effort. Its charge was to "get the cost down."

Clarifying the Request

The team studied documentation to determine what processes and practices were in place (including the point-of-purchase sales process, purchasing and customer service practices, and vendor qualification process). They observed the overall system. They conducted open interviews with management to learn their vision, mission, and to determine the company's interfaces with internal and external customers and vendors. A structured interview was used and the entire staff was surveyed. Interview questions included the following:

- Is the overall POP sales process cost-competitive?

- Is the process well run and efficient?

- What are opportunities to reduce costs?

- Does the process add value to the overall system?

Understanding the Current System

Current process sketches

The following diagrams are sketches the team made of two major processes at Beta Corp.: the order-to-collection and POP purchasing and sales processes. (See Exhibits A and B.) The sketches provided the team with a rough overview of how the processes function, with notes attached describing issues, timelines, costs, and so on. The POP purchasing and sales process diagram shows the major activities, timelines, and concerns. The order-to-collection process diagram shows all the relevant departments, functions, and subcontractors and how they interrelate.

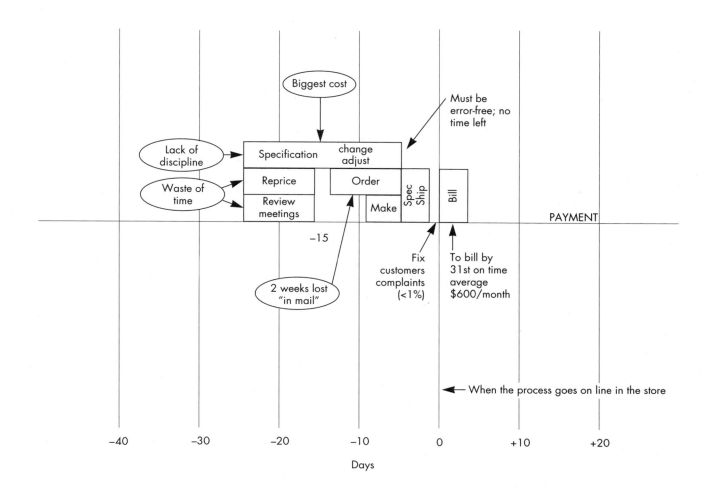

Exhibit B: Order-to-Collection Process

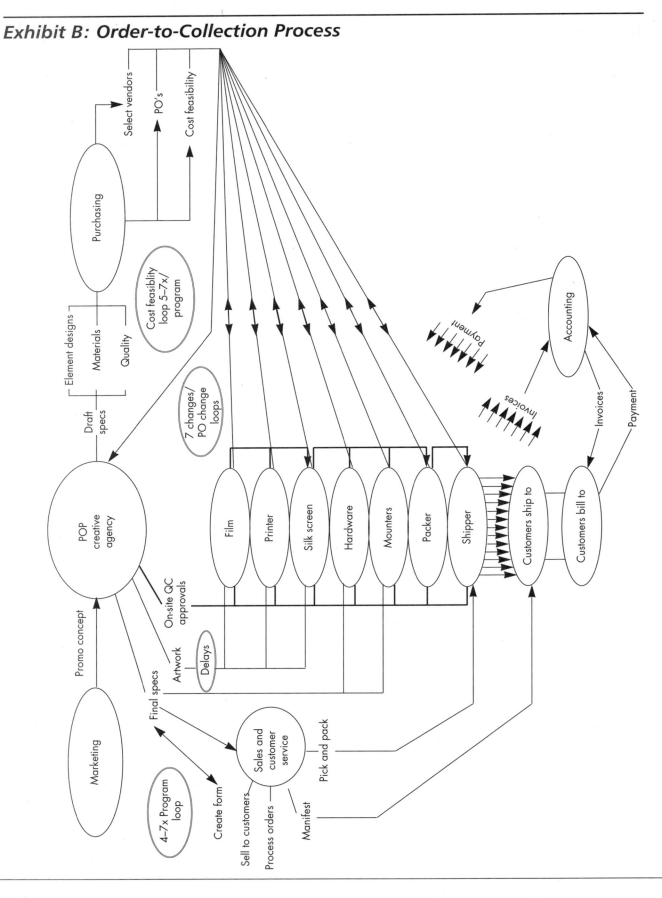

Analysis of the overall process: Order to collection

The following is an issue-by-issue analysis of what the team learned about the process:

- Beta employees, vendors, and customers dislike the waste of time in the current order-to-collection process.

- Despite the complex reviews and approval process, creative inputs are changed right up to the time the job is run.

- Each breakdown forces everyone downstream in the POP process to exert extra effort and spend extra funds to meet the delivery deadline.

- The POP process is not designed to provide good customer feedback in time to make a difference. This leaves customers and vendors alike feeling powerless to improve the process and its outcomes.

- There are complaints about short order lead times, inflexible kits with extraneous or inappropriate elements, insufficient outdoor support, and poor store execution.

- Vendors complain about short lead times, lack of creative discipline and accountability, and tearing down and setting up jobs just to satisfy a person's ego.

- Customers are wary of complex programs and order extra pieces to cover the errors they expect. One agency complained that POP cost estimates are consistently too low.

- The POP group is holding up the POP programs. This has negative impact on local sales. For example, POP was supposed to be available 1/1/93, but so many changes were made it was April before the material was available. Three months of opportunity were lost.

- Information consistently degrades as it moves through the product creation-to-distribution process.

- Elements in complex POP programs change many times. Order forms may be redrafted five to fifteen times before they can be sent to customers in the field. Good information is critical to improving cost and quality consistency.

- One symptom is that customers and vendors do not know who to call about POP programs, so they call the general number. They then complain if the staff member does not know the information they seek or if they are transferred.

- Vendors must constantly reshuffle key people, equipment, and materials to respond to delayed inputs.

- Beta is never allowed to delay delivery.

Evaluation of key production and distribution activities

The team identified the following key production and distribution processes and how they could be improved:

- Purchasing kit components from qualified vendors: value added could be improved; clean turnovers would improve efficiency; current on-press approvals are inefficient.

- Scheduling production and distribution to meet the system's delivery requirements: value added could be improved; incomplete turnovers cause delays and extra charges.

- Job tracking to ensure that quality requirements and schedule requirements are met or exceeded: value added could be improved.

- Cost tracking: required process, could be improved; 7.5 change orders issued per purchase order.

- Pick and pack: value added improvement planned for the future.

- Shipping tracking: required process, could be improved.

- Managing inventory: required process, could be improved.

Evaluation of the billing activities

The team walked through the billing process. This is what they learned:

- System artwork is released by a creative agency. Beta accepts or rejects it on behalf of vendors.

- At actual press time a person from the creative agency goes to the press and approves the proof. The press waits until he makes approval.

- Every time there is a delay that costs money above the original bid, the vendor calls Beta and asks for a change request. The purchasing manager approves the change and a clerk issues the change request. Copies go to the vendor. For example, the vendor sends Beta a $50,000 invoice on an original bid of $46,000. Billing has to go through all change orders (on paper) and make sure they all add up to the invoice total. Billing hopes the invoice covers only one job. If it doesn't balance, it goes to Purchasing and Purchasing sends it back to the vendor. Also, the billing person interfaces with two different computers on two different platforms. Billing receives an average of 7.5 change orders for every purchase order.

- Beta has a policy that all shipped items must be billed in the month shipped. If there are any shipment delays, nine thousand bills may have to be sent out in only one or two days. The window of opportunity is compressed.

- If bills were sent on a monthly basis, it would reduce paperwork by 60 percent. The chief financial officer likes the current system because he can look at data on a monthly basis and he doesn't have to carry any inventory. However, this procedure is driving up costs for no valid business reason.

Creating a New Design

After the team had analyzed the current system, they determined that by implementing three recommendations management could reduce costs.

1. Create a preliminary pricing matrix to price POP commodities. Beta must negotiate prices for standard kit commodities that will remain valid for a specified time period. (See Exhibit C.) This will eliminate Purchasing's involvement in the cost feasibility loop, which happens three to seven times per program for each of the twenty-two programs, at eight to sixteen hours per cycle. This will save time, keep pressure off downstream vendors, and therefore decrease errors and overtime.

2. There must be "clean turnover." The creative agency must meet artwork/layout/keyline deadlines with all art completed.

   - If inputs are delayed, the agency must make up the time. The product must ship on schedule.

   - If the artwork is incomplete on some elements of the kit, you can't see the whole kit to check its effectiveness and quality.

   - The kit can't be packed until all the elements arrive at the packer. Therefore, noncritical artwork must be eliminated.

   - Changes to specifications or artwork after final approval by Marketing increases costs by increasing overtime and increasing errors. It also increases the business risk of downstream vendors, driving their quotes up, giving them no time for environmental problem identification, and causing them shipping delays.

3. Automate and streamline the entire order-to-collection process.

   - Make a preorder convert automatically to an order when released (with or without edits).

   - Simplify the process by completing activities in parallel. (See Exhibit D.)

   - Check edits on numbers, items, subtotals, and totals. If all are OK, then invoice. This would eliminate manual matches on hard copy and filing of paperwork.

The team concluded that by focusing on these three recommendations, management could close the performance gap.

Exhibit C: Costing (Price Feasibility) Matrix

By Vendor

Kit Item	50–99	100–249	250–999	1,000–4,999	5,000–10,000
A	$20	$18.50	$17	$15.50	$14
B					
C					
D					
E					

By Item

Kit Item	Vendor 1	Vendor 2	Vendor 3	Vendor 4	Vendor 5
50–99 A	$20		$22.50		
100–249 A	$18.50		$20.00		
250–999 A	$17		$18.50		
1,000–4,999 A	$15.50		$14		
5,000–10,000 A	$14		$12.50		

Exhibit D: Completing Activities in Parallel

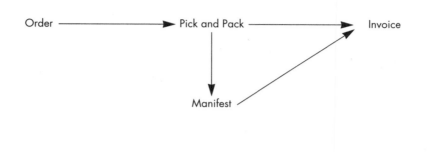

Implementing the New Design

Many of the team's recommendations were implemented, and the results to date have been very promising. For example, a new role for the buyers has been defined. Many of the manual filing and tracking systems have been computerized. Implementation did not happen overnight, and certain glitches did appear. However, by having strong management support, and open and honest dialogue about the problems and how they affect performance, and by giving people the necessary resources to solve the problems, the implementation went as smoothly as possible.

Success factors

Some of the key success factors of this redesign are similar to those presented in Chapter 6:

- Strong executive support
- Adequate groundwork for change
- Constant communication
- Redesigning openly, not trying to hide the effort
- A small, core redesign team and help from experts
- Adequate resource commitment

SECTION FOUR

RESOURCES

Overview

This section provides you with various resources to help you redesign processes (specifically, worksheets for gathering and organizing data). You can either copy the blank worksheets or use them as a basis for designing your own worksheets.

One word of caution: These worksheets are paper-based (since this is a book). You can increase the efficiency of your data-gathering efforts if you use a computer to immediately capture what you learn. You can easily adapt the resources provided here for use on a computer.

Project-planning or activity-based software is often quite comprehensive and flexible, allowing you to input data into a structured, yet manipulatable format, and giving you the ability to export data to other software packages.

Resource A: Critical Issue Worksheet
Part 1—Interview

Directions: Use the cues below to jog your memory, and use Procedure 2.1 as a guide.

What are the specific results or outputs that are not being achieved?

_____

How do you know this is a problem? Are there any specific metrics that indicate this is a problem?

_____

If this were no longer a problem, how would you know? What would be the relevant indicators? How would you know it was solved, specifically?

_____

What customers were concerned?

_____

What does the customer say he or she wants? Why is this important to the customer?

_____

What do you think our customers expect that they have not said? Why is this important to the customer?

_____

What do you think would excite our customers? Why is this important to the customer?

_____

Who are the customer's customers, and what do they need to be successful?

_____

Why is this output important to you?

_____

What do you believe would be the impact of closing this gap on our customers and on the organization?

_____

Is this critical business issue linked to the strategic plan? How?

_____

What is the best process to redesign to address the critical business issue?

Will this process have an impact on our customers?

Can this process be redesigned?

Will redesigning this process affect overall unit performance? How?

In redesigning this process to close the performance gap, will we need to redesign incrementally or fundamentally?

Part 2—Current Process Sketch

Draw or sketch a rough draft of the process. Identify the major outputs of the organization and where they go. Identify the major inputs and where they come from. Draw how the different functions (marketing, design, etc.) convert the input into the output. Keep thinking of the entire system as a series of inputs and outputs. The output of one function is the input to another.

Resource B: Design Team Charter Worksheet

Directions: Use the template below and Procedures 2.2, 2.3, and 2.4 as a guide.

Critical Business Issue: _____

Process: _____

Sponsor: _____

Steering Committee Members: _____

_____

_____

_____

_____

_____

_____

Redesign Team Members: _____

_____

_____

_____

_____

_____

_____

_____

Resource C: Current Process Worksheet

Directions: Use the format below and Procedures 3.4 and 3.5 to summarize your findings about the current process. You could also use this worksheet to look at organizational culture (Procedure 3.1).

Theme	Frequency Heard (rare, some-what rare, sometimes, often)	Populations	Unique?	Comments

Resource D: Current Culture Survey

Directions: Use the sample questions below and Procedure 3.1 to summarize your findings about the current organizational culture.

How open is the culture to new ideas?

_____

How much analysis is expected before a group of managers or executives will champion a new idea?

_____

Are people willing to change?

_____

Are there certain critical variables that convince people that change is necessary more than other variables do?

_____

What is the risk tolerance of the culture?

_____

How conservative is the culture fiscally and elsewhere?

_____

How have radically new ideas been introduced, if ever, in the past?

_____

What are the culture's basic assumptions regarding risk, change, analysis, safety, and openness?

_____

Who are the heroes? What makes them heroes (e.g., inviting change, encouraging innovation, taking risks)?

_____

What gets celebrated? Innovation?

_____

What are the rites and rituals around conformity?

_____

Who gets promoted?

_____

To get ahead, is it more important to be political and posture or to do what is best for the business and its customers?

_____

How much time is spent doing activities for activity's sake versus achieving results?

_____

What percentage of your decisions do not need approval or a signature from anyone else?

_____

How candid can you be about issues?

_____

What has happened to people who have been direct, open, and completely honest about issues?

_____

Are people measured on results or on completing many activities?

_____

Is this organization driven by people's obtaining results or by their "looking like" they are obtaining results?

_____

Do you believe it is easy to get things accomplished, or that there is too much bureaucracy?

_____

Resource E: Financial and Human Resource Systems Analysis Survey

Directions: Use the guide below and Procedures 3.2 and 3.3 to summarize the key issues about the current financial and human resource systems.

List your ideas about five major financial issues that could affect the successful implementation of the redesign.

1. _____

2. _____

3. _____

4. _____

5. _____

List your ideas about five major human resource issues that could affect the successful implementation of the redesign.

1. _____

2. _____

3. _____

4. _____

5. _____

Resource F: Process Analysis Worksheet
Part 1—Understanding the Current System

Directions: Use the checklist below to determine if you have finished collecting all of the data about the current process. Use Procedures 3.4 through 3.10 as a guide.

Have you ...	Yes or No
Sketched the core process?	
Determined the main output(s) of this process?	
Sketched or listed the tasks that make up each activity?	
Charted the flow of information?	
Charted the use of technology?	
Identified where activities occur?	

Resource F: Process Analysis Worksheet
Part 2—Current Performance Data

Directions: Use the table below to understand how the process is currently performing. Use Procedure 3.9 as a guide.

Activity	Length of Time to Perform the Activity and Achieve the Output of the Activity (Process Time and Cycle Time)	Resources Needed (People, $, Etc.)	Comments

Resource F: Process Analysis Worksheet
Part 3—Current Success Factors and Roadblocks

Directions: Use the table below to understand the success factors of the current process. Use Procedure 3.10 as a guide.

What factors are contributing to the success of the current process?	Why?	What causes these factors?

(continued on next page)

What factors impede the success of the current process?	Why?	What causes these factors?

Resource G: Customer Needs Worksheet
Part 1—Redesign Team Survey

Directions: Use the questions below and Procedure 4.1 to help you confirm customer needs.

Who are our current customers?

_____

Who are will be our customers in five years?

_____

Customers				
How profitable?				
How much revenue is generated by this customer?				
What percent of our overall sales goes to this customer?				
Will this customer be strategically important to us? Why?				
Who are this customer's suppliers?				
Who are this customer's customers?				
Strengths?				
Weaknesses?				
Competitive threats to this customer?				
Market share in each operation to which we sell our products?				
Overall financial performance?				
Customer's problems and concerns?				
Customer's growth potential?				

Part 2—Customer Survey Summary

Customer Name _____

Primary or Secondary Customer?_____

	1	2	3	4	5	6
	Answer	Why is the answer in column 1 important?	Why is the answer in column 2 important?	Why is the answer in column 3 important?	Why is the answer in column 4 important?	Why is the answer in column 5 important?
What the customer says he or she wants						
What you think the customer expects that was not said						
What you think would excite the customer						

Resource H: Worksheet for Choosing Incremental or Fundamental Redesign

Directions: Answer "yes or no" to the questions below using Procedure 4.2 as a guide. The more "yes" answers there are, the more likely that fundamental redesign should be considered.

Question	Yes or No
Is the level of improvement required considered a paradigm shift?	
To achieve the goal, will the organization need to operate under different assumptions?	
Is the bureaucracy considered overwhelming and stifling?	
Are people operating in silos?	
Are there many problems in the execution of this cross-functional process?	
Even by improving every step in the process, would we not reach our goal?	
Does the organization's culture need to change?	
To achieve the improvement, will other systems and departments (i.e., HR, Finance) need to change?	
Are we on a "burning platform" (is the business in major trouble)?	
Is the process fragmented? For example, is no one accountable for the entire process? Do items get thrown over the wall to the next operation or function?	

Resource I: Accomplishments and Activities Worksheet

Directions: Fill in the table below, using Procedure 4.3 as a guide. Using an activity-based software program or a spreadsheet will make calculating totals and summarizing data much easier.

Accomplishment/ Output	Activity	WAIT Category	Process Time	Cycle Time (min.)	Cycle Time (max.)	Cycle Time (avg.)	Cost. ($ min.)	Cost ($ max.)	Cost ($ avg.)	Dept. or Function	Responsible	Technology	Comments

Resource J: Performance Gap Analysis Worksheet

Directions: Use the questions below and Procedure 4.4 to help you determine performance gaps.

Accomplishment			
Desired performance			
Actual performance			
Gap (if any)			
Significance of gap			
Is gap critical? Why?			
Root cause			
Best alternative			
Can or will an activity be eliminated?			
Job(s) affected			
Activity category			

Resource K: Cost/Benefit Analysis Worksheet
Part 1

Directions: Complete the tables below, using Procedures 4.7 and 4.14 as guides.

Alternative	Financial Benefits	Nonfinancial Benefits	Financial Costs	Nonfinancial Costs
Total				
Total				
Total				

Part 2

Criteria/ Constraints	Alternative A		Alternative B	
	Yes	No	Yes	No
Total				

Resource L: Implementation Worksheet

Directions: Use the table below, Resource J, and Procedure 5.1 to help you implement the new re-design.

Accomplishment			
Desired performance			
Actual performance			
Gap (if any)			
Significance of gap			
Is gap critical? Why?			
Root cause			
Best alternative			
Can or will an activity be eliminated?			
Job(s) affected			
Actions to close the gap			
Responsibility			
Completion date			

References

Andrews, D. C. and Stalick, S. K. *Business Reengineering: The Survival Guide*. Englewood Cliffs, N.J.: Yourdon Press, 1994.

Bardwick, J. M. *Danger in the Comfort Zone*. New York: AMACOM, 1991.

Beer, M., Eisenstat, R. A., and Spector, B. "Why Change Programs Don't Produce Change." *Harvard Business Review* (November–December 1990): 158–166.

Beer, S. *Brain of the Firm*. New York: Penguin, 1972.

Beer, S. *Diagnosing the System for Organizations*. New York: Wiley, 1985.

Bridges, W. *Managing Transitions*. Reading, Mass.: Addison-Wesley, 1991.

Daniels, W. R. *Group Power I: A Manager's Guide to Using Task Force Meetings*. San Diego: Pfeiffer, 1986.

Daniels, W. R. *Group Power II: A Manager's Guide to Conducting Regular Meetings*. San Diego: Pfeiffer, 1990.

Davenport, T. H. *Process Innovation—Reengineering Work through Information Technology*. Boston, Mass.: Harvard Business School Press, 1993.

De Bono, E. *Serious Creativity*. New York: Harper Business, 1992.

Dewar, R. D. and Dutton, J. E. (1986). "The Adoption of Radical and Incremental Innovations: An Empirical Analysis." *Management Science*, 1986, *32* (11), 1422–1433.

Duck, J. D. "Managing Change: The Art of Balancing." *Harvard Business Review* (November–December 1993): 109–118.

Eisenhardt, K. "Speed and Strategic Choice: How Managers Accelerate Decision Making." *California Management Review*, Spring 1990, *32*, 39–54.

El Sawy, O. A. and Khershid, H. S. *A Design Theory of Virtual Workflows*. Research Paper IOM 94–13. University of Southern California, July 1994.

Eureka, W. E. and Ryan, N. E. *The Customer-Driven Company*. Dearborn, Mich.: ASI Press, 1988.

Fields, R., Taylor, P., Weyler, R. and Ingrasci, R. *Chop Wood Carry Water*. Los Angeles: Jeremy P. Tarcher, 1984.

Gabarro, J. J. *The Dynamics of Taking Charge*. Boston, MA: Harvard Business School Press, 1987.

Galbraith, J. R. *Organization Design*. Reading, Mass.: Addison-Wesley, 1977.

Gerken, G. *Abschied vom Marketing.* Düsseldorf, Germany: ECON Verlag, 1990.

Gibb, J. *Trust.* North Hollywood, CA: Newcastle Publishing, 1991.

Goal/QPC. *The Memory Jogger: A Pocket Guide of Tools for Continuous Improvement.* Methuen, Mass.: Goal/QPC, 1988.

Goldratt, E. *The Goal.* Croton-on-Hudson, N.Y.: North River Press, 1984.

Hall, G., Rosenthal, J., and Wade, J. "How to Make Reengineering Really Work." *Harvard Business Review* (November–December 1993): 119–131.

Hamel, G. and Prahalad, C. K. "Strategic Intent." *Harvard Business Review* (May–June 1989): 63–76.

Hamel, G. and Prahalad, C. K. "Strategy as Stretch and Leverage." *Harvard Business Review* (March–April 1993): 75–84.

Hammer, M. "Reengineering Work: Don't Automate, Obliterate." *Harvard Business Review* (July–August 1990): 104–112.

Hammer, M. and Champy, J. *Reengineering the Corporation.* New York: HarperCollins, 1993.

Harrison, R. "Understanding Your Organization's Character." *Harvard Business Review* (May–June 1972): 119–128.

Jaques, E. *Requisite Organization.* Arlington, Va.: Cason Hall, 1989.

Juran, J. M. *Juran on Quality by Design.* New York: Free Press, 1992.

Kaplan, R. B. and Murdock, L. "Core Process Redesign." *McKinsey Quarterly,* 1991, *2,* 27–43.

Katz, D. and Kahn, R. L. *The Social Psychology of Organizations.* New York: Wiley, 1966.

Langeler, G. H. "The Vision Trap." *Harvard Business Review* (March–April 1992): 46–55.

Lawler, E. E. *The Ultimate Advantage: Creating the High Involvement Organization.* San Francisco: Jossey-Bass, 1992.

Leeds, D. "The Art of Asking Questions." *Training and Development* (January 1993): 57–62.

Lewin, K. "Group Decision and Social Change." In T. Newcomb and E. Hartely (eds.), *Readings in Social Psychology.* New York: Holt, Rinehart & Winston, 1947.

Lincoln, Y. S. and Guba, E. G. *Naturalistic Inquiry.* Newbury Park, Calif.: Sage, 1985.

Mackenzie, K. D. "The Process Approach to Organizational Design." *Human Systems Management,* 1989, *8,* 31–43.

Meyer, C. "How the Right Measures Help Teams Excel." *Harvard Business Review,* May–June 1994, *72(3),* 95–103.

Miller, J. *Living Systems.* New York: McGraw-Hill, 1978.

Mintzberg, H. *Mintzberg on Management.* New York: Free Press, 1989.

Morris, D. and Brandon, J. *Reengineering Your Business.* New York: McGraw-Hill, 1993.

Northey, P. and Southway, N. *Cycle Time Management.* Cambridge, Mass.: Productivity Press, 1993.

Pasmore, W. A. *Designing Effective Organizations—The Sociotechnical Systems Perspective.* New York: Wiley, 1988.

Perrow, C. *Organizational Analysis.* Belmont, Calif.: Wadsworth, 1970.

Phillips, D. *Lincoln on Leadership.* New York: Warner Books, 1992.

Porras, J. I. *Stream Analysis: A Powerful Way to Diagnose and Manage Organization Change.* Reading, Mass.: Addison-Wesley, 1987.

Porter, M. E. *Competitive Strategy.* New York: Free Press, 1980.

Prahalad, C. K. "The Core Competence of the Organization." *Harvard Business Review* (May–June 1990): 79–91.

Putz, B. [Johann, B.] "Guidelines to Constructing Evaluation Instruments." In F. Stein (eds.), *Instructor Competencies: The Standards.* Batavia, Ill.: International Board of Standards for Training, Performance, and Instruction, 1992.

Rummler, G. A. and Brache, A. P. *Improving Performance.* San Francisco: Jossey-Bass, 1991.

Ryan, K. D. and Oestreich, D. K. *Driving Fear Out of the Workplace.* San Francisco: Jossey-Bass, 1991.

Schaffer, R. H. "Demand Better Results and Get Them." *Harvard Business Review* (March–April 1991): 142–149.

Schaffer, R. H. and Thomson, H. A. "Successful Change Programs Begin with Results." *Harvard Business Review* (January–February 1992): 80–89.

Senge, P. M. *The Fifth Discipline.* New York: Doubleday, 1990.

Shapiro, B. P., Rangan, V. K. and Sviokla, J. J. "Staple Yourself to an Order." *Harvard Business Review* (July–August 1992): 113–122.

Smith, P. G. and Reinertsen, D. G. *Developing Products in Half the Time.* New York: Van Nostrand Reinhold, 1991.

Spadaford, J. F. "Reengineering Commercial Loan Servicing at First Chicago." *National Productivity Review* (Winter 1992–93): 65–72.

Srivastva, S. *Executive Power.* San Francisco: Jossey-Bass, 1986.

Stalk, G., Evans, P., and Shulman, L. E. "Competing on Capabilities: The New Rules of Corporate Strategy." *Harvard Business Review* (March–April 1992): 57–69.

Stolovitch, H. D. and Keeps, E. J. (eds.). *Handbook of Human Performance Technology.* San Francisco: Jossey-Bass, 1992.

Tichy, N. M. and Sherman, S. *Control Your Destiny or Someone Else Will.* New York: Doubleday, 1993.

Tomasko, R. M., *Rethinking the Corporation: The Architecture of Change.* New York: AMACOM, 1993.

Turney, P. *Common Cents.* Hillsboro, Ore.: Cost Technology, 1991.

Umbaugh, R. E. *Handbook of IS Management.* Boston: Auerbach, 1991.

Umbaugh, R. E. *Handbook of IS Management: 1993–1994 Yearbook.* Boston: Auerbach, 1993.

VanGundy, J. A. B. *Techniques of Structured Problem Solving.* New York: Van Nostrand Reinhold, 1988.

Walker, R. Rank Xerox—Management Revolution. *Long Range Planning, 25* (February): 7–21.

Weinberg, G. M. *Rethinking Systems Analysis and Design.* Boston: Little, Brown, 1982.

Wheatley, M. J. *Leadership and the New Science.* San Francisco: Berrett-Koehler, 1992.

Wurman, R. S. *Information Anxiety.* New York: Doubleday, 1989.

Index

A

Accomplishments: current process and, 56; defining critical business issue and, 3, 5; definition of, 114; identifying, for new design, 114–116, 128; new design evaluation and, 130, 136; worksheet for, 214
Activity-based costing (ABC), 89
Activity-based software tools, 58, 77
Adaptability, and changing business conditions, 4
Adding value, 134
Allocation, 67
Altering (A) activity, 114, 115, 129
Artifacts, in organizational culture, 62
Assumptions, in organizational culture, 62, 63
Authority: in fundamental redesign case study, 180; implementation and, 149; new design and, 135; organization chart and, 143, 144; of sponsor, 39; of steering committee, 43

B

Barriers to implementation, 156–160
Beer, S., 6
Beliefs, in organizational culture, 62, 64–65
Benchmark: critical business issue and, 35; definition of, 122
Benefits of new design, 141
Boundaries of core process, 35
Brache, A. P., 8, 9, 77, 119–120
Brainstorming, 106; communication vehicles and, 53; financial costs of alternatives, 125; identifying performance gaps with, 117; root cause determination with, 119; techniques for, 122–123

Brandon, J., 58, 77
Breakthrough thinking, 132–133
Budgets, in current financial system, 69
Bureaucracy: mechanistic model and, 5; new process design and, 134; responses to changing business conditions by, 4
Business conditions, responses to changes in, 3–4
Business organizations: implications of new organizational models and, 6–7; need for understanding current processes in, 15–16; phases of Process Redesign Model in, 10–18; process view of, 7–10; responses to changing conditions by, 3–4
Business process design: building case for, 3–20; rationale behind, 1
Business strategy: goals of redesign efforts and, 11; redesign effort and need for, 14
Business Week, 3

C

Case studies: fundamental redesign, 163–188; incremental redesign, 189–197
Cause-and-effect diagram, 119, 121
Champy, J., 5, 11, 15
Change: barriers to, 157; communication and, 50; risk and, 106; success of redesign efforts and managing, 20
Charter of redesign team: definition of, 39; in fundamental redesign case study, 164, 167; goals of redesign efforts and, 11; sponsor and, 41; success of redesign efforts and, 19; worksheet for, 202

Clarifying the request, 11–14, 32–54; choosing redesign team members and, 44–47; communication vehicles for, 50–54; defining critical business issue and, 34–38; framework for redesign team and, 48–49; fundamental redesign case study and, 164; incremental redesign case study and, 190; sponsor and, 39–41; steering committee and, 42–43; success of redesign efforts and, 20

Common framework, 48–49

Communication: creating vehicles for, 50–54; fundamental redesign case study and, 164, 187, 188; implementation and, 18, 152, 153, 154; success of redesign efforts and, 19, 20

Communication plan: definition of, 50; implementation and, 154; steps for developing, 52–53

Compensation system: in current system, 73; in new design, 139

Core cross-functional process: defining critical business issue and, 34, 35, 37; sketch of, 77–79; verifying process map of, 95–96

Cost accounting, 67, 68

Cost plus, 67

Cost-to-benefit analysis, 125, 141–142, 146; worksheet for, 216–217

Costs: of current processes, 56; of development delay, 129; identifying accomplishments and, 115; mechanistic model and, 5; new design and, 129, 141; performance measures with, 90, 91; responses to changing business conditions and, 4; trade-offs in redesign efforts and, 13–14

Creating the new design, 17, 103–147; choosing a redesign methodology for, 111–113; customer needs and, 108–110; fundamental redesign case study and, 177–178; incremental redesign case study and, 195–197; "outside the box" thinking in, 103, 106; recommended approach to, 105

Creativity: brainstorming and, 122; "outside the box" thinking and, 103, 106

Critical business issue: current financial system and, 68; definition of, 35;

fundamental redesign case study and, 165–166, 169; goal of redesign effort and, 11; new design evaluation and, 136; performance gap analysis and, 117; procedure for defining, 34–38; root cause determination and, 120; worksheet for, 200–201

Critical success factors: for current process, 93–94; redesign efforts and, 19–20

Culture, organizational: choosing incremental or process redesign and, 112; in fundamental redesign case study, 170–172; understanding, 62–66; worksheet for, 204–205

Current processes, 15–16, 55–101; environment for activities in, 87–88; executive summary report on, 100–101; financial system and, 69–72; fundamental redesign case study and, 166, 168–169; human resources (HR) systems and, 71–76; incremental redesign case study and, 190–194; information flows in, 82–83; listing tasks for activities in, 80–81; organizational culture and, 62–66; performance data on, 89–92; points to be determined for, 56; sketching core process in, 77–79; software for modeling, 58; success factors in, 93–94; technology use in, 84–86; verifying map of, 95–99; worksheet for, 203, 207

Customers: analysis of current processes affecting, 15, 16; creating a new design and needs of, 108–110; current process outputs and, 56; · defining critical business issue and, 36; in fundamental redesign case study, 177–178; identifying, 108; implementing a new design and, 18; new design evaluation and, 134–135; performance gaps and, 117; redesign team membership and, 45; reengineering approaches and focus on, 10; success of redesign efforts and, 19, 20; worksheets for, 211–212

Cycle time, 89, 91, 115

D

Data collection: on current financial systems, 68–69; defining critical business issue and, 36–37; organizational culture survey for, 63, 64–65; redesign position paper and, 51, 52

Davenport, T. H., 8

De Bono, E., 132

Decision making: in current business processes, 15; mechanistic model and, 5; new design and, 135, 145

Disagree and commit paradigm, 50, 51

Diversifying, 4

Downsizing, 4

Duck, J. D., 18

E

Economic conditions, responses to changes in, 3–4

Effectiveness factors, 129–131

Efficiency, and new design, 134

Elapsed time, 90, 91

Environment: definition of, 87; identifying, for flowchart, 87–88

Evaluations: of best alternative to performance gaps, 125–126; of new design, 141–142; of performance, 72

Examples: choosing the best alternative to performance gaps, 126; cost-versus-benefit chart for new design, 142; current financial system data collection, 70; current process success factors, 94; customer interview, 109–110; defining critical business issue, 38; environment for activities, 88; executive summary report, 101; financial system changes for new design, 138; flowchart of core process, 79; generating alternatives to performance gaps, 124; human resources system changes for new design, 140; human resources system data collection, 76; implementation Gantt chart, 154; information flowchart, 83; objectives of new design, 129; organizational culture data collection, 66; performance data measurements, 92; performance gap analysis worksheet, 118; redesign position paper, 54;

redesign team membership, 47; root cause determination with fish-bone diagram, 121; sketching tasks in an activity in a process, 81; summary sheet of accomplishments, 116; technology use flowchart, 86; verifying a process map, 97–99

Executive summary report: definition of, 100; preparing, 100–101

Executives: current financial system and, 68–69; goals of redesign efforts and, 11; implementation and, 157; presentation of new design to, 147–149; steering committee and, 43; success of redesign efforts and, 19, 20. See also Top management

Expectations: goals of redesign efforts and, 11; sponsor and, 41; of top management, 14

F

Facilitator, 49

Fantasy, in breakthrough thinking, 132

Fifth Discipline, 10

Financial system: in current system, 69–72; in fundamental redesign case study, 173; implementation and, 153; in new design, 137–138; survey of, 173, 206

Fish-bone diagrams, 58, 121

Flexibility: changing business conditions and, 4; in fundamental redesign case study, 181

Flowcharts, 58; core process on, 77–79; identifying environment on, 87–88; information flow on, 82–83; as iterative process, 77; listing tasks for activities in, 80–81; technology use on, 84–86

Focus groups, 16

Format: of executive summary report, 100, 101; of presentation on new design, 146

Formative feedback, 9

Free association, 122

Fresh look technique, 132

Fundamental redesign; breakthrough thinking in, 132–133; case design of, 162, 163–188; choosing, for new design creation, 111–113, 213;

clarifying goals of, 11; confirming objectives and effectiveness factors in, 129–131; critical success factors in, 19–20; definition of, 111; evaluating new design in, 141–142; executive and steering committee presentations on, 147–149; financial system changes needed for, 137–148; human resources system changes needed for, 139–140; incremental redesign compared with, 12; organization chart in, 143–144; as part of continuum, 105; Process Redesign Model phases and, 25–26; sketching the new process in, 134–136

G

Gantt chart, 152, 154, 155
Gerken, G., 4
Goal/QPC, 119, 120
Goals of redesign effort, 11; choosing redesign team members and, 44–47; sponsor and, 39–41; steering committee and, 42–43; success of redesign efforts and, 20

H

Hammer, M., 5, 9, 11, 15
Human resources (HR) systems: in current system, 71–76; in fundamental redesign case study, 173; implementation and, 153; in new design, 139–140; survey of, 173, 206

I

Implementation, 18, 149–160; barriers to, 156–160; creating plan for, 152–155; in fundamental redesign case study, 187–188; in incremental redesign case study, 197; managing, 154; sponsor and, 39; worksheet for, 218
Incremental measurement, 9
Incremental redesign: case design of, 162, 189–197; choosing, for new design creation, 111–113, 213; clarifying goals of, 11; critical success factors in, 19–20; definition of, 111; determining best alternative in,

125–126; determining root cause in, 119–121; executive and steering committee presentations on, 147–149; fundamental redesign compared with, 12; generating alternatives in, 122–124; human resources system changes needed for, 139–140; identifying accomplishments and categorizing activities in, 114–116; identifying performance gaps in, 117–118; as part of continuum, 105; Process Redesign Model phases and, 25–26; sketching the improved process in, 127–128
Inertia, organizational, 4, 6
Information flow: charting, 82–83; in current process, 56; in new design, 128, 136, 139
Information systems: human resources systems and, 75; new design and, 135
Inspecting (I) activity, 114, 115, 129
Integration, and new design, 135, 187
Interviews: charting information flows with, 82; charting technology use with, 85; choosing incremental or process redesign, 112–113; of customers, 109–110; on current financial system, 68–69; on current human resources system, 72–75; defining critical business issue with, 36; fundamental redesign case study and, 164; organizational culture survey for, 63, 64–65; verifying process map with, 96
"Is map," 9

K

Kaufman, R., 9, 10

L

Lewin, K., 6

M

Machine model, 5
Mackenzie, K. D., 6
Managers and management: current financial system and, 68–69; fundamental redesign case study and, 166, 187; implementation and, 18, 149,

154, 157; new process design and, 134; process view of organizations and, 7; sponsor and, 39; success of redesign efforts and, 20; training for, 74. *See also* Top management

Margin, 67

Mechanistic model, problems associated with, 5

Mental model of organizations, 6

Metrics: in current process, 56; defining critical business issue and, 34, 35

Models: changing business conditions and need for new, 5; choosing software for creating, 58; implications of new approaches to, 6–7; importance of relationships and interdependencies in, 6; older approaches to, 5

Morris, D., 58, 77

N

Network models, 58

Newton, I., 5

O

Objectives of new design, 129–131

Organization chart, 143–144

Organizational culture: choosing incremental or process redesign and, 112; in fundamental redesign case study, 170–172; understanding, 62–66; worksheet for, 204–205

Organizations: culture of, 62–66; inertia in, 4, 6; mental model of, 6; systemic conceptualization of, 10. *See also* Business organizations

Outputs of current processes, 56; flowchart of, 79; identifying, 114–116; new design evaluation and, 136; objectives of new design and, 130; performance measures with, 90, 91; sketching tasks in an activity with, 81

"Outside the box" thinking, 103, 106

P

Paradigm, definition of, 50

Performance data: measures used for, 90, 91; procedure for determining, 89–92; root cause determination

with, 119; sponsor and, 41; worksheet for, 208

Performance evaluations, 72

Performance gaps: choosing best alternative to, 125–126; definition, 117; generating alternatives to, 122–124; identifying, 117–118, 128; worksheet for, 215

Performance management plan, 67, 68–69

Performance management system: in current system, 72; in new design, 139

Physical environment, and core process, 77

Pilot, and implementation, 152

Plans: implementation, 152–155. *See also* Communication plan

Position paper. *See* Redesign position paper

Problem: critical business issue and, 35, 36; fundamental redesign case study and, 168

Process: approaches to improving, 9; definition of, 7; fundamental aspects of, 8

Process attributes, 35; in fundamental redesign case study, 180–182

Process control, 9

Process improvement techniques, 9–10

Process map, 9, 77; in fundamental redesign case study, 183–185; new design with, 128; performance data and, 89; verification of, 95–99

Process measures, 132

Process owners, 143, 149

Process redesign: ways of becoming involved in, 27. *See also* Fundamental redesign; Incremental redesign

Process Redesign Model, 10–18, 25–160; clarifying goals in, 11–14, 32–54; comparison of incremental and fundamental redesign and, 25–26; creating the new design in, 17, 103–147; implementing the new design in, 18, 149–160; phases of, 10; understanding the current system in, 15–16, 55–101

Process time, 89, 91, 115

Processes: examples of, 15; interdependencies between, 6, 20; maps of, 9; need for understanding current, 15; organizations viewed through, 7–10; systems composed of, 1

Productivity: mechanistic model and, 5; new design and, 129; responses to changing business conditions and, 4

Profit and loss (P&L) statement, 67

Project management software, 58

Prototypes, 17

Q

Quality: new design and, 129, 134; as performance measure, 90, 91

Quality control techniques, 9

Quantity of output, 90, 91

Quantum world model, 5

R

Rangan, V. K., 95

Recurring processes, examples of, 15

Redesign: building case for, 3–20; changing business conditions and need for, 3–4; implications of new organizational models and, 6–7; key factors for success in, 19–20; management support for, 13–14; Process Redesign Model in, 10–18, 25–160; process view of organizations and, 7–10. *See also* Fundamental redesign; Incremental redesign; Process Redesign Model

Redesign position paper: definition of, 50; example of, 54; executive summary report and, 100; guidelines for, 51; presenting, to executives and steering committee, 147–149; steps for creating, 52–53

Redesign team: choosing members of, 44–47; common framework for, 48–49; communication vehicles and, 53; creativity of, 103, 106; definition of, 44; example of, 47; fundamental redesign case study, 164, 167; group process of, 49; implementing a new design and, 18; understanding current processes and, 15, 16

Reengineering: case for, 9; customers and, 10

Resource costs, as performance measure, 90, 91

Resources, 199–218

Restructuring, 4

Reversals, 132

Review gates, 182–183

Risk: beliefs about, 64; change and, 106

Root cause: definition of, 119; determining, 119–121; performance gap and, 118

Rummler, G. A., 8, 9, 77, 119–120

S

Scope of redesign effort, 34; in fundamental redesign case study, 179–185

Senge, P., 9, 10, 106

Shapiro, B. P., 95

Size of organization, 4

Sketches: advantages of, 78; of core process, 77–79; in incremental redesign case study, 190–192; of new process, 127–128, 134–136

Skill levels: in current system, 75; in new design, 139

Smith, P. G., 129

Software: implementation and, 152; modeling processes with, 58, 77

Sponsor: critical business issue and, 34, 35, 37; definition of, 39; in fundamental redesign case study, 180; goals of redesign efforts and, 11; implementation and, 149; incremental or process redesign choice and, 112–113; procedure for choosing, 39–41; redesign position paper and, 52; steering committee and, 43; success of redesign efforts and, 19, 20

Steering committee: choosing members for, 42–43; definition of, 42; presenting new design to, 147–149

Strategic Planning Plus, 10

Success factors: for current process, 93–94; in fundamental redesign case study, 188; in incremental redesign case study, 197; redesign efforts and, 19–20; worksheet for, 209–210

Summary sheet of accomplishments, 115–116

Surveys: of customers, 212; of financial and human resource systems, 173, 206; in fundamental redesign case study, 171–172; of organizational culture, 63, 64–65

Sviokla, J. J., 95

System-oriented thinking, 132

Systemic thinking, 10

Systems: analysis of current processes using, 16; processes composing, 1

Systems analysis, of current processes, 15, 16

Systems model, 5, 6

T

Target costing, 67

Task: charting information flows with, 82; definition of, 80, 82; listing, for each activity in a process, 80–81; performance measures for, 91–92

Team leader, 39; implementation and, 149; sponsor and, 41

Teams: in fundamental redesign case study, 180; on organization chart, 143. *See also* Redesign team

Technology: charting use of, 84–86; in current process, 56; definition of, 84; identifying, for new design, 115; in new design, 128, 136

Technology-enhanced thinking, 132

Time commitments: of redesign team members, 46; of sponsors, 39

Top management: choosing incremental or process redesign and, 112–113; communication vehicles and, 50; cost-to-value trade-offs in fundamental redesign and, 13–14; implementation and, 18, 152, 157–158; sponsor and, 39

Training in process redesign, 49

Training systems: in current system, 74; in new design, 139

Transition team, and implementation, 18

Transporting (T) activity, 114, 115, 129

Tree diagrams, 58

Troubleshooting techniques, 9

Trust: organizational culture and, 65; redesign efforts and need for, 14; success of redesign efforts and, 19

Turney, P., 91

V

Values and beliefs, 62

Van Gundy, A. B., Jr., 122, 125, 132

Virtual Management, Inc., 58

Visual imagery, 132

W

Waiting (W) activity, 114, 115, 129

Warnier-Orr diagrams, 58

Weinberg, G. M., 16, 78

"What If" technique, 123, 132

Wheatley, M. J., 5, 6

Wishful thinking, 132

Work force skills: in current system, 75; in new design, 139

Workflow BPR, 58

Worksheets: accomplishments and activities, 186, 214; choosing incremental or fundamental redesign, 179, 213; cost/benefit analysis, 216–217; critical issues, 165–166, 200–201; current culture, 204–205; current performance data, 175, 208; current process, 170, 203; current success factors, 176, 209–210; current system, 174, 207; customer needs, 177–178, 211–212; design team charter, 167, 202; determining best alternative to performance gaps, 126; fundamental redesign case study use of, 165–166, 167, 170, 174–176, 177–178, 179, 186; implementation, 218; performance gap analysis, 117, 118, 128, 215; process analysis, 207–210; redesign team summary, 211